Dreams Lost and Found

My Life As A Chauffeur

Morris Bussie Jr.

authorHOUSE

AuthorHouse™
1663 Liberty Drive, Suite 200
Bloomington, IN 47403
www.authorhouse.com
Phone: 1-800-839-8640

© 2009 Morris Bussie Jr.. All rights reserved.

No part of this book may be reproduced, stored in a retrieval system, or transmitted by any means without the written permission of the author.

First published by AuthorHouse 5/1/2009

ISBN: 978-1-4389-6578-9 (e)
ISBN: 978-1-4389-6576-5 (sc)
ISBN: 978-1-4389-6575-8 (hc)

Printed in the United States of America
Bloomington, Indiana

This book is printed on acid-free paper.

Cover photos by Benjamin Kyler © Cozion Media (202) 577-6991

ACKNOWLEDGEMENTS

First and foremost, to my higher power and dream giver Almighty God.

Then to the woman that told me I could do anything I put my mind to the first woman in my life my mother "Benzina Colemen." I love you so much.

Next the man that stepped into my life and gave up his life for mine my stepfather Ronald Colemen, "rest in peace."

To my sister, Laura, Rhonda, and Kathy, who was always a source of inspiration.

To my Pastor and mentor Pastor Rev. St.Clair Mitchell.

Morris Bussie Jr.

To my sons Bryant, Morris, Marty, and Micheal Bussie. And to my grand daughters, Morrisa, Monasa and Monik.

And to the first mentor in my life, the man that helped to make sense of many things in my early years Mr. Crowder. To Sarah Lee Smith thanks for your encouragement.

To the one person I adore, the love of my life, my beautiful wife and friend, Sylvia.

Last but not least, the persons that help me put this book together Delores Forbes, thank you.

CONTENTS

Acknowledgements	v
Introduction	1
"From Where I Started"	5
"The Move to Washington"	17
"Responsibility of Life"	25
"Almost Lost It"	35
"Life Changing Experience"	47
"My Wildest Experience as a Chauffeur"	61
"Hanging with the Stars"	81
"Working with Royalty"	103
"People That Have Made a Difference in my Life"	129
"The Weekend with his Royal Badness"	133
"My Turn"	161

Introduction

This book is about humble beginnings, lost dreams, distractions, recovery, rules to live by things to believe in and people that have made a difference. Why it's impor- tant to have integrity, to find your place and be true to your cause. To live your life to be an inspiration that others will have hope and believe in their dreams because with out a dream life has no challenges.

Always have a dream!!

This is a story about my life where I started and where I've been.

Morris Bussie Jr.

My story started back in Philly, Mr. Crowder, my friend's father, would always say, "you have to look like somebody." Those words have always stuck in my mind. He believes in order to get people attention they had to see you first. I can remember one of the old heads back in Philly, when he used to tell me, "Little Brother" everyday that you wake up, you're in school. You never stop learning, but it's what you do with what you learn that makes the difference.

When you see me I'm dress in a crisp black suit, white shirt, silver tie, wearing a pair of semi paten loafers on my feet. I always look the part of a professional.

When I glide through the streets in my big black Sedan Limousine, the people on the street would turn their head and watch me and wonder, "who is that." I only nod my head to them and keep on driving because I'm a professional at all times. It's also important that I look the part at all time.

I have driven here and there, and I always check out the spots before time. I have work with P. Diddy, Mary J. Blige, Prince Bandar, Mr. Clarence Cazalot, Rubin, and many more......

When I was a young teenager back in Philly, my dreams were to become a musician but somewhere along my journey I got distracted. But as I got older I realize I should have

Dreams Lost and Found

never given up on my dream. But being around successful people has influenced my life. I have always studied them. Now I have new dreams.

Hold on to your dream, and if you lose one, another dream is just around the corner.

"From Where I Started"

"First you have to look like somebody." Those were the words of my friend father, Mr. Crowder. He believed in order to get peoples attention they had to see you first. And then you had to earn there respect by the way you carry yourself. That one simple rule never left me and I carry it with me every day. Looking back on my early years, growing up in Philadelphia I was impressed by people that everyone else wanted to know. At the age of seven I remember living in North Philly on a little street called Sterner Street. The street was so small that people had to park on the sidewalk in order for other cars to get by.

Morris Bussie Jr.

On the corner of our street was a small storefront church, that's where I first met Teddy Pendergrass. I didn't know who he was at the time because I was only seven years old and that was before he became a star. It was something about him back then, everyone new he would be a great singer. He was the lead singer in the church choir and when he sang people would shout and cry. From that moment on I knew what I wanted to do. I wanted to make people scream, clap, and be happy, also. One night while standing on the outside of the church after a choir rehearsal he came out looked at me and said, "why aren't you at home doing your homework little man?" I just gazed at him and said, "I wanted to hear the music." He patted me on my head and said, "so you like music." Yea! I said. Well in order to be a good musician and singer you have to study and get your education. At an early age I was always drawn to greatness and people who got things done. I liked how people gathered around them and how they would smile and be happy. Growing up in North Philadelphia for the first eight years of my life was tuff on our family, my father left my mother when I was about two years old. My mother was strong, and determined to give us a good home. There were three children my oldest sister Laura, my brother Benjamin, and me.

Dreams Lost and Found

When my mother met my step father Ronald Coleman I was about three years old. I will always appreciate my step father for stepping into our lives when we needed a father and a male figure around. I could never understand how my real father could leave my mother with no money, no job, and three small children to take care of. But I guess that's another book I have to write. Before moving from North Philly I got a taste of just how bad it was out in the streets.

I can remember one day the Diamond street gang and a gang called Zulu Nation were fighting. My mother called us all in the house, but me being the adventurous one after coming in the house, I went and opened up the window to look out, my friend next door, was still sitting on the steps. One of the gang members came down the street and stabbed my friend in his legs. The next week Ronny moved us up to West Oak Lain. Back then in the late sixties that was considered the suburbs. The house we moved from was small compared to our new house. The new neighborhood seemed to be a lot safer. I was a little older and learned to be more independent.

The new house had three bedrooms, and a basement. I had to share a room with my brother. That's where I spent most of my time listening to the radio and playing music. Everyday I dreamed of becoming a musician and a singer. I always had an outgoing personality, I liked talking to people and making them feels good. In Junior High School I became popular. I was a quick study of people, fashion, and music. Some of the actors I liked at the time were Billy D. Williams, Sidney P. and Fred Williamson.

Dreams Lost and Found

I had been bugging my mother for a guitar for the longest, so for Christmas she and Ronny bought me one. I learned to play it in about three months. Jimmy Hendrix was one of my favorite guitar players along with Santana and some others. So I listened to their albums and I learned how to play them note for note. All through junior high school I became more and more popular for my musical abilities, and the way I dressed. At that time somewhere deep inside of me, I knew that I had to look the part of someone in order to be somebody.

After meeting my friend, Steve in my second year of Junior High School we became close friends. If I wasn't at his house he was at mine. Steve wasn't a musician but we did other cool things together. He was just a cool person to be around. After I met his father and he told me, "son in life, first you have to look like somebody before you can become someone. It's like he had been in my life sense the beginning. Sometimes God puts people in your life for a reason. That's why Steve and I got along so well. It was almost like we were brothers. I will never forget the Crowder family.

I also found out in life that the first imprecision is a lasting, imprecision but it's what you do and say afterward that counts. Something else I found out from one of the old heads in the neighborhood was never let an opportunity get by without trying to grab hold of it. He said, "some people

Morris Bussie Jr.

miss that one opportunity that could change their lives for the better." Never be afraid to take chances. The people in Philadelphia seemed more outgoing and warm. The old heads would talk to us about trying to be successful in life.

After being in West Oak Lane for a while I found out that we lived around a lot of stars. We lived on 67th avenue. Right around the corner on Oqontz Avenue is where the heavy weight champion of the world Joe Frazier lived. I remember in school I was cool with Joe Frazier's son Marvis. But I didn't know who he was at the time. One day after school Marvis asked me to come walk home with him so I could see his new bike. When we reach his house my eyes lit up. The house was bright red. When we went inside, I could not believe that we were in the same neighborhood. We walked through his living room. Every where I looked was glass chrome and mirrors. The house was laid out. We went downstairs and that's when I realized that I was in Joe Frazier's house. There were pictures of famous fighters, trophies, and championship gloves every where. It was like being in a museum. After about fifteen minutes, Joe Frazier walked down stairs. I could not believe it. Then my instinct took over, I walked over to him put out my hand and said, "hi Mr. Frazier I'm Morris, Marvis's Friend." Right away I showed my respect and in return I gained his. Success in life

Dreams Lost and Found

is giving others respect, that builds relationships for a life time.

To this day Mavis and I are still friends. I have not heard from him in years, but I know whenever we see each other we are still cool. Celebrities are human just like everyone else. They like their privacy but they also like to be appreciated for what they do. So when ever I met a celebrity, I'd walk up to them and introduce myself and say something positive. That way if you ever see them again they'll remember you. Just like what Mr. Crowder said, "first you have to look like somebody, but after they see you say something intelligent and they will never forget you. Even after meeting thousands of other people, you'll stand out."

Patti LaBelle also lived in our neighborhood. I met her one day outside of a grocery store. As a young man I was crazy about her, but I didn't want to walk up to her like a giddy school boy, so I gathered my composure, walked over to her and said, "hi Ms. LaBelle she turned around and said hi baby. How are you doing with your little handsome self?" After that I didn't know what else I said but she laughed and said ok sweetie bye bye.

At some point in our lives, we have some sort of indication of what we want to be in life. That day I became sure of what I wanted to become in life. At a young age I knew that I was destined to be in the entertainment industry in one way or another. I began to work even harder. My mother and friends could not believe how much my guitar playing and my vocals improved. My last year in Junior High School, I found a job working in a diner after school so I could buy my own clothes. In the seventies the look was silk, and wool pants, white Chuck Taylor sneakers, and two tones knit sweaters. The musicians wore platform shoes, bell bottom pants, and tie died shirts. I had two wardrobes, one for each mode. I was known for the way I dressed and how I carried myself and that made me feel good about who I was becoming. I knew I was on the right track.

After working in the diner for about two weeks, guess who comes in, but Patti LaBelle. I couldn't believe that she remembered who I was but she did. She also remembered where she had met me. I thought back to what Mr. Crowder had said again, "Look like somebody and say something intelligent and they'll never forget you. After Patti LaBelle left the diner she gave me my first big tip $30.00. Back in the seventies at the age of fifteen that was a lot of money. Since that day in the diner I was known as the guy who knew Patti LaBelle. I had everyone's respect from that day on.

Later that year I decided to form a band. I found a drummer, base player, piano, and some percussion. The name of the group was called L7. At first we sounded terrible. No

Dreams Lost and Found

one in the group had experience playing with anyone before. So we had to learn to play as a group. Three weeks went by and we finally sounded pretty good. The first song we learned was Sisco Kid by War.

My first year in high school I realized how important it was to be cool and popular not only by the other kids but with the teachers as well. I was sixteen years old and I was beginning to stand out more and more. It was clear to me what I wanted to be in life. All I had to do was stay focused and stay out of trouble. One of my teachers Mr. Moor said, "I was and old man in a young mans body." Some of the seniors didn't like me because I was a tenth grader who was already popular. It felt very good to be someone, people wanted to be around me.

My friends Steven Crowder, P-nut, Dead Eye, Earl, Lacy, and Chubby, were like family. Steve's father Mr. Crowder was the man we could always learn something from. He had something positive to say whenever we talked to him. He reminded me of the guy that patted me on the head years ago in my old neighborhood, which later I found out was Teddy Pendergrass. We go through life sometimes not realizing how much we can learn from other people. Just by listening and keeping an open mind. Somehow that found its way into my soul and spirit as a child and it stayed there. I want to be the best person I can be at all times.

After a few months our group built up a pretty good repertoire of music and was ready for our first show. The first time we performed was a learning experience. We were rushing through the songs. The vocals were too loud and we were nervous. Like the old saying goes "Rome wasn't built over night." We had a lot of work to do, but we all were willing to work hard. We would go to see other groups perform and we studied there stage presents and how they interacted with the crowd. Before long it all came together. One Friday night we performed at Temple University and we had all of our friends there to support us.

We told everybody we knew. But by the time the show started the promoter came to us and said, "oh by the way W.D.A.S. Radio station will be here doing some promotions." When we herd that we knew it was a chance to really show what we had. The MC came to the stage, the lights went down and we all were ready and in our places on stage. The MC introduced us and the crowd started screaming. We started playing Percussions first, and then all of sudden we broke into Cisco Kid. The crowd went crazy.

That experience for me was one of the high lights in my life. The way it made me feel was like I could accomplish anything if I put my mind to it. I was learning more and more, that along with looking like somebody, I had to also know something. So I studied the music industry and some

Dreams Lost and Found

of the local artist, because if I met someone in the industry I would be educated. Back then I wanted to make all the right moves and stay around the people I knew could help me get to the next step in the music industry.

Some people have a hard time trying to figure out where they want to go in life but I knew exactly where I wanted to go. At the beginning of my senior years, all kinds of thing were happening, drugs, girls, and cutting classes. All kinds of negative distractions, Danny the drummer of the group was killed in a car accident. Sammy the rhythm guitar player joined the army. Lacy the base player, became hooked on drugs. Earl moved to L.A. And the girl I was seeing at the time said she was pregnant. In one year everything went down hill. After high school was over in 1977 and the band had broken up, Earl moved to L.A. and I began to work as a trash man back in Philly.

I hated getting out of bed every morning and going to a job that I didn't like, but it made me realize that sometimes things happen for a reason. It makes us stronger. It shows character when we can go through something and still be positive about where we are going in life. I have never lost my dream of being in the entertainment industry. In a lot of ways I'm thankful for going threw hard times. It makes you appreciate what you get when it comes.

Morris Bussie Jr.

Working as a trash man was good for a few reasons, one was the exercise and I got in great shape. It also made my vocals so clear because I sung a lot as I work. A few weeks went by then Earl called me from L.A. "Hey man if you know what I know you better come to L.A. on the next thing smoken, this is the place to be for musicians. So I made plans to move to L.A. I saved some money within a few weeks but it wasn't enough. So I called my father who was living in Maryland with my step mother and two step sisters. I asked him if I could come to visit for a while. He said yeh ok.

My intentions was to go and ask for a loan to get to L.A. so

I quiet my job as a trash man and I told my mother that I was going to visit my dad in Maryland for awhile. I didn't tell her I was going to L.A. because I didn't want to hurt her. My mother was my best fan. She wanted the best for us. I wanted to someday be able to have my mother retire in style and not have to want for nothing. She and my step father worked hard for us to get what we needed. They sacrificed there whole life for us. So I wanted them to be happy.

"The Move to Washington"

I left Philadelphia and came to The Washington D.C. area in the summer of 1977 to visit my father and stepmother Ruth and two stepsisters. My Intentions were to get a loan from my father then move on to Los Angeles CA. My homeboy Earl had moved to L.A. earlier that year, but stayed in touch with me. Earl was a go getter, just like I was, when we started our group back in Philly. We made a promise to each other that whoever made it first, would come back for the other. When I got to Washington to visit with my father, I couldn't bring myself to ask for enough money to move to LA. At the time my father was a minister at a church on 14TH Street in Washington D.C.

Morris Bussie Jr.

They invited me to go to church one Sunday and I excepted. When Sunday came I was up and ready to go. My stepmother was a musician at the church, and she knew that I also was a musician and played guitar. When she told me I might be able to sit in with the orchestra I was excited. When we arrived at church all I wanted to do was go where the musicians were setup. I went over and sat down next to the musicians. This church was very unusual. Later during the service my father introduced me to the church. My stepmother told the congregation that I was a musician also. That Sunday, I was able to play with the orchestra. After church I asked my father if we could stop, so I could buy a newspaper to find a job.

That night I found a job at Wheaton Plaza in a men clothing store. Wheaten Plaza was a mall that I herd about that had 100 stores. I worked at Embassy father and son as a salesman. It was the perfect job for me at the time. I got a 15% discount off my clothes. There was a tailor who also worked at the store we became a good friend. Then later he taught me to sew. After awhile I became a tailor myself. A few months went by and I was still in Washington. I managed to save some money, but needed about six hundred dollars more. Meanwhile, I still attended church every Sunday with my father and stepmother. After one Sunday service my step

Dreams Lost and Found

mother came to me and asked me, what do you think of the young ladies at the church?

I said what do you mean? She said, "there are a lot of young ladies asking about you." They ask me if you have a girlfriend. At the time all I was thinking about was making it to L.A., where my homeboy Earl was and doing good working on his music career. At the time that's all I was interested in. The next Sunday my stepmother introduced me to a young lady after church was over. She asked her to come to the house for dinner. She said O.K. My stepmother was working hard to find me a girlfriend I really didn't understand because I told her that I was preparing to move to L.A. I became very annoyed with her, but remained a gentleman.

Now more than ever I wanted to get to L.A. After we came home, I called Earl in L.A. I ask if he had any money he could send me. Earl said, "things were tight for him in L. A." He was living in a one bedroom apartment that was very expensive, and he was only working four days a week as a studio musician. He felt bad that he couldn't help me, but I understood. I was so angry with my stepmother. My father was always low key he didn't say much about what I was trying to do.

When dinner was over I walked the young lady to her car, and we made plans to meet for lunch two days later.

Morris Bussie Jr.

The young lady name was Charlene, and she was a nice looking lady, but very domineering. In my heart, I knew that she wasn't my type, but I continued to go out with her. I don't know what it was or why I just didn't say to her I don't think we are compatible. It may have been because she had a good job, her own car, and an apartment. That is where we spent a lot of time. I should have run as fast as I could when I told her what my dreams and goals were, and she just dismissed it, just like I didn't say anything. She was strictly a church girl....with no room for anything else. I have always been taught that God helps those who help themselves. So anything that I dreamed I could do, God would help me accomplish it.

In early 1978 I was still in Washington, and trying to figure out what was happing in my life. I was confused and frustrated. All I wanted was to follow my dream of becoming a musician and entertainer in Los Angeles. Some of the things I learned up in Philly was to "go for it," Be the best that you can be, you can do it. I'm not putting down the church, I just couldn't understand why "this church" wasn't motivating anybody, and the pastor was telling all the young people to get married instead of following their dreams, or getting an education, so that they could first be able to take care of themselves. Well in February of 1978, I was the next unprepared young person to step into a life of overwhelming

Dreams Lost and Found

responsibility. I wasn't ready for it. To this day I don't know why I did.

I throw away the chances I had of making it to L. A. When I called my real mother, who was back in Philly, she couldn't believe what I had done. Why did you do that? She said, "You are too young for that." When I sat down and thought about what I had done, and the real reason I did it. The only thing I could say was I wasn't thinking for myself. It was the people around me I let them make the most important decision of my life. The next thing I knew we were having our first son, at the age of nineteen I could barely take care of myself. I was so angry with myself. My whole personality changed. Why was everyone so in a hurry for me to get married, except me, and why did I do it? Only God knows why. Before I got married I was living with my father and step mom. The only reason I could think of why they wanted me to get married was to get me out of the house. I told them that I wanted to save my money and move to L. A. It would have only taken three more months to save the money that I needed. I had fallen into the same trap that the other young people of the church. I got married before I really knew who I was.

Having major responsibilities to soon in life can make you bitter and unhappy. I remember something I learned from Mr. Crowders, when I was living in Philly, he said,

Morris Bussie Jr.

"don't rush your life." If you follow your dreams and don't get distracted you'll be happy everyday of your life. Well I was distracted "Big time." I moved to a place where it seemed that everyone was afraid to believe that dreams do come true. I always had faith in my ability to be what ever I thought I could be. Later on in life I found out that you have to surround yourself with people that think the same way you do. You have to have an open mind, because life is not one dimensional.

When I called my home boy Earl in L. A., he couldn't believe what I was telling him. He listened to me and didn't say a word. Then he called me every "stupid ass" in the world. Man what are you thinking about? Why did you do that? How are you going come to L. A. now? You just messed up man and he hung up the phone. Earl was the only one I could depend on. All my life and up until now I was the only one he could depend on. So here I am in Washington, D.C. married with a son.

My life wasn't happening the way I planned it. My best friend wasn't talking to me. My mother in Philly was devastated, my oldest sister from Philly was mad. It really hurt everyone that knew me and knew what I was capable of becoming all of a sudden I got married. It felt like I was stuck in a time warp and instead of going forward I was slowly moving backward. Now instead of being a carefree

Dreams Lost and Found

"nineteen year old" that was following his dreams, I was a married man with a family to support.

A big lesson I had to learn in life is, don't listen to other peoples opinions about your life, and what they think you should be doing with it. Don't let their opinions take you off the path to fulfilling your life and happiness. Only you and God know, what that path is!!

"RESPONSIBILITY OF LIFE"

After the birth of my first son, Morris III, I knew that I had to be totally committed to him. After all, I grew up without my father around so I wanted to be there for my son. Having children makes a person become responsible really fast!! It can be a dream killer, because you no longer have yourself to think about but another human life. My life was totally different. All of my freedoms were gone. I began to hate my life and everything about it. When I would pray to God and ask him to show me what to do, I always saw my sons face! I didn't understand why at first, then I came to "Realize" that what he was telling me to do was stay in my son's life and raise him. Sometimes when I think I made the wrong decision about getting married, I tell myself that God wanted

Morris Bussie Jr.

me to have my children by this woman, that's the only thing that made sense. I loved her, but I don't think I was in love with her. She was a strong woman, very domineering and opinionated, so I guess those would be good traits to pass down to our children. We were so different in every way. I was a dreamer and believed that anything was possible. "Just don't put limits on yourself." She was strictly a church girl, she didn't believe in taking risk. She always played it safe. I on the other hand, would try anything to make a change for the better. Not saying that she wouldn't, but she had limitations. Two years after Morris III was born we had another son, Marty. I was now working as a manager of a formal wear store in downtown Washington. I started as an Assistant Manager but quickly moved up to manager. We went to church every Friday night and Sunday mornings. We seamed like the perfect family, but deep down inside I couldn't help but think, what my life would be like if I had moved it to L. A. We lived in an apartment in Suitland MD.

At the time we both worked in downtown Washington so we would commute together everyday. Our sons were born on the same day, but two years apart, that made it easy when birthdays rolled around It felt good to be apart of my sons life, but there was something inside of me that wanted more out of life. I had been with the church choir and orchestra since I came to Washington in 1977, but deep down in my heart that's not where I wanted to be. An old head back in

Dreams Lost and Found

Philly once told me, "never let an opportunity get by you without trying to grab hold to it." I never forgot what he said. When I let the opportunity to go to L.A. get by, I felt that I missed my calling.

My sons have brought so much joy to my life and I couldn't imagine being without them. In 1983 our third son was born, after the birth of Marty, Charlene had her tubes tied, but somehow got pregnant again. Michael was born on November 25th. All of our sons were born right around the holidays, which made it more difficult financially. My weekly salary as a manager was barely enough to support a wife and three children. Charlene also worked for the telephone company. The only outlet I had from work and my responsibilities at home was church. I would have never believed years ago, that I would be a church man, but that's how fast your life can change.

Besides being apart of the church choir and orchestra, I was also a member of the group "Norris Gardner" and company. Music was still a big part of my life. Every chance I got to sing or play my guitar, I took it. The group traveled all over Washington D.C., North Carolina, Virginia and Baltimore. We also recorded an album in a local studio.

As time went by our sons developed their own personalities, but they all had one thing in common, they were all talented. Morris, the oldest, learned to play the drums. I can remember

Morris Bussie Jr.

when he was just a baby sitting him on my lap, as I practiced playing the drums, he loved to watch me, then try to imitate what I was doing. Marty was more laid back. He developed a strong baritone singing voice.

Michael was the smart one. We found out when he was in the first grade, that homework was never a problem for him, even the hardest math problems were no match for Mike. Their mother and I always kept them active. When Michael, the youngest turned six years old I started a dance group with the three of them. I would choreograph all of their dance steps and their mother coordinated their clothes. They became known all over Washington as the "Bussie Boys." They danced at Howard University, and at birthday parties. They were the opening act for Be.Be. and Ce.Ce. Winans, at the J. W. Marriott in Washington, D.C.

Dreams Lost and Found

One thing I always told them, it was the same thing that I learned when I was just a young man growing up in Philadelphia, from one of my mentors Mr. Crowder. I told them "first you have to look like somebody." Then you have to earn peoples respect by the way you carry yourself. I have lived with that belief all my life, and found that when you give respect, you get respect, and people will remember you whenever they see you again. In life sometimes it's not what you know, but it's who you know.

When I first got married in 1978 I didn't know what I was getting myself into. Know one sat me down and talked to me about the responsibility of raising children, or having a wife. I became angry and bitter on the inside but I was determined not to let it damage my personality. I didn't want to be known as a person with a bad disposition. So I never let my bitterness show, I held it in and that almost lead to self destruction.

After working as a store manager for about two years, we were able to save some money, so that we could buy a house in Oxon Hill Maryland. Our sons were older and needed more of our time. We didn't want them to get caught up in the streets, or in peer pressure. Every Friday night and Sunday morning, we had then in church. When we didn't have church, I had them practicing on their dance steps. In 1988 after living in Oxon Hill for a year I decided to

Morris Bussie Jr.

change jobs. I found a job closer to our house in Temple Hill Maryland. It was a Tailors position. I learned the art of tailoring from "Lenny Solouter." He was the Tailor from the first job I had when I moved to Washington, At Embassy father & son. Lenny became a good friend. He taught me perseverance, and to always be willing to learn new things. Lenny was maybe the only one who I could talk to about what I was going through. His life had played out almost in the same way, after he moved from Jamaica. Lenny helped me through the first year of my marriage.

Everyday, when I arrived at work, I would go down to the tailor shop and talk with Lenny and he would teach me the trade. I learned from him, if you're in a place where you don't want to be, keep an open mind, because you can learn something from every situation. Who would have known that I would have become a tailor. I worked as a tailor for a formal wear shop in "Temple Hills" Maryland for four years.

In 1991 while working there, I also became an entrepreneur and started a small Tuxedo business in the basement of our house. At first it started slow maybe a few weddings a month, then it started to grow from word of mouth. Before I knew it, I was doing six or seven weddings in one month. During Prom season, April, May, and June I became so busy it was hard to keep up.

Dreams Lost and Found

Something very important happened to me that year! I learned that I could be a success if I worked hard enough at it. Although I wasn't a star in L. A., or had records playing on the radio, I had become a success in life by trying to be the best at what ever I put my mind to. The Tuxedo business was doing so well that I wanted to open up a store. I knew it would be a great opportunity to start a family business, and have something to pass down to our children. I knew in my heart and soul that starting a business would work because I had already established a clientele. People had trust in me knew that and I would deliver when I said I would. I began preparing for the next step in making this dream a reality.

I went out looking at different locations, where a formal wear shop might do well. However, when you are married you have to consider what your partner thinks about your vision and your goals for the future. I have always believed in taking chances, but this time was different. The business was already making money and growing everyday. All we needed to do was expand by moving into a building that could accommodate the business. I talked to my then wife, about how this would improve our lives and secure the future for our children, but she couldn't understand. She thought it was too big of a risk.

"I believe life is just like school, you go from one grade to the next. As the saying goes "God helps those who help

Morris Bussie Jr.

themselves," A lot of people have a hard time understanding what that means. We spend so much time praying for God to bless us and give us everything we need, that we don't realize everyday he gives us the power to do, be and have everything we want. Fear is the one thing that can kill dreams, and keep us in a constant state of confusion, always thinking of a better life but never willing to take a risk, and watch God work it out. After all the work, all the research, and all of the planning there was nothing to stop us but us. My wife was so set against us opening our store that it made me withdrawn and angry.

To think my wife didn't have enough faith in me, as the head of the household, by understanding that all I wanted to do was make a better life for us. After all, we pray and ask God to bless us, and when he does, if it takes working a little bit in order to get what we ask for, we think that it's not for us. In life we can have all the faith in the world, but if we are not willing to work hard for it, we will not get it. The Bible tells us, "faith without work is dead." We all want to be in good health, or financially secure, but if we don't work on it, it will not happen.

As a married couple we had different ideas, as to how blessings worked. The longer we were married the more I learned just how much different we were. "Eventually I gave up the idea in order to keep the peace at home. "Never let

Dreams Lost and Found

an opportunity get by without trying to grab hold to it." By this time in my life, it had become a habit for me to get right to the blessing and then give up, because I let myself be talked out of it. Right now in my life I'm supposed to be a wealthy man. The biggest downfall in my life is being a people pleaser. Over the years I have learned to listen to God first, then follow my instincts. I believe I can do anything I put my mind to. I have never had fear of anything, because what I learned as a young man growing up in Philly, has never left me.

"We have to take control of our lives by making the right choices for ourselves." Don't let other people tell you that it can't be done, "Be persistent, don't let other people talk you out of your dream." But most of all don't talk yourself out of it."

"Almost Lost It"

After giving up the second biggest dream of my life, I felt useless. I knew that I could do anything I put my mind to. "So what was the problem?" My dreams were dying, one after the other, every time I would get right to the door of my blessing, I would let people tell me that I couldn't do it. After I gave up on the idea for the Formal Wear shop, my whole attitude changed. I began to drink and run with the wrong crowd. Life was "torture" for me. I knew I was supposed to be a business owner, but who was I going to blame, myself, or the people who thought I was crazy to want to open the first African American Formal Wear shop in the Washington area.

Morris Bussie Jr.

In November of 1992, my life started slowly going down hill. I was depressed everyday, mad, unproductive, and for the first time in my life, I didn't have a dream. I felt like every other working stiff, getting up every morning, and going to a job to make just enough money to pay my bills. It was torture, because I knew I could do better, "much better." I always had a fight on the inside, a drive and determination that made me want to be more than an ordinary person. Eventually I gave up the Formal Wear business all together. I just didn't want to do it if I couldn't do it right.

By April of 1993, I was drinking everyday I just didn't care about anything. At this point, all I wanted to do was feel good. I was still working as a tailor at the Formal Wear shop in Temple- Hill M.D. I also joined a gym that was close to my job. Everyday for lunch, I would go to the gym and workout. It became a good way to relieve my frustration.

One day after I left the gym, I ran into an old acquaintance, that used to live in an apartment complex that we moved from. His name was Steve. He was from Cleveland Ohio. We would see each other at the swimming pool and share stories about where we grow up. Steve was also a singer and had moved to Washington hoping to further his music career. We exchanged numbers and promised to keep in touch. One Friday night Steve called and invited me over. That was one time I wished I had never answered the phone. When I got

Dreams Lost and Found

to his house and rang the bell, Steve came to the door and his eyes where blood red. He said, "come on in and join the party. We went into the dinning room, it was just Steve and his wife sitting at the dinning room table. They had been drinking beer and smoking weed, while playing cards. They looked to be enjoying themselves. They asked me to sit down and join them, I said sure why not. After all, I had smoked a little weed back in Philly, so it was no big deal. While sitting there for awhile, I noticed a glass bowl, and I said, that bowls a little small for weed isn't? Steve's wife said, "it's not for weed, and picked it up and dropped a small white rock in it, put it to her mouth and lit it. Steve turned to me, and asked have you ever tried rock before? No man! I said and I ain't about to. Steve and his wife began to laugh uncontrollably. When they finally stopped, he looked at me and said, "man I know you not scared?" My brother, let me tell you something, I know all about that sh---- so what do I have to be scared of. I held up the joint and said this is all you need.

We continue to play cards, and they continue to put the little white rock in the bowl. My instincts was telling me to go home, but my curiosity got the best of me. It was now about ten o'clock, they looked like they didn't have a care in the world. Steve turned to me once again and said, "come on man try this. Without hesitation, I got up and walked to

Morris Bussie Jr.

the door. Steve said, "hay man are you leaving?" Yeah! I will call you tomorrow and walked out. Everything I have heard about "Rock" was not good, but it seemed like everybody was doing it.

In my life it was always important for me to be around the right people. So I started thinking, were they the right people to be around? I needed something in my life to make me feel productive, outside of going to the gym, I didn't do much else. I had stopped going to church, which had become a part of my life after coming to Washington. I would never put a church down or talk bad about it, but it wasn't where I belonged, and I knew it. I started visiting other churches and found one in Fort Washington M.D. The minister always had a positive message. It seemed like he was talking directly to me. He always encouraged the congregation to work for themselves. He would tell us, "open your own business." I felt like my soul was being fed.

No one really knew how devastated I was, when I didn't take the opportunity to open up the Formal Wear shop. It made me start believing in myself again. To hear someone else tell me I could do anything I put my mind to. Every Sunday I couldn't wait to get to church and hear the minister's encouraging messages.

Dreams Lost and Found

My wife couldn't understand why it was so important for me to be at this church. She said to me, "Morris a church is a church." I said no, the church that's good for you, might not be good for me. We were so different in every way, but we respected each others opinions. Things were tense at home, my wife and my children were going to a different church than I. It seemed like the family was going in two directions.

As each day went by, I became more and more frustrated and depressed. I started thinking of all the dreams I have had and the goals that I never reached. I remembered what my mentor, Mr. Crowder once told me back in Philly, he said, "son, always have a dream." That is the one thing nobody can take from you. At this point in my life, it seemed like I couldn't even by a dream. I felt empty. It was now the forth of July weekend 1993, I received a call once again from Steve to invite me over for a cookout. He said, "there were some people he wanted me to meet, and some of them were musicians. I wasn't to particular about hanging out with Steve or his wife, but I thought it was a good opportunity to meet other musicians, and maybe get a chance to promote myself.

I arrived at Steve houses around four thirty. People were everywhere, children were running and having a good time and there were people in the swimming pool. There were

Morris Bussie Jr.

about three card games going on and the music was blasting. It was a totally different mood from the first time I visited them. Steve and his wife was the perfect host this time. I felt so relaxed and at home. Steve's wife walked me through the cookout and introduced me to everyone as a friend of the family.

I was surprised to see that they knew all types of people from all walks of life. There were a couple of young ladies from Philly, that went to the same high school as I. When they found out, we hung together the rest of the evening talking about old times back in Philly.

It was getting to be around nine o'clock most of the people who had small children had gone home to put their children into bed. The rest of us went inside, where we continued playing cards and hanging out.

Steve found me, and we met the musicians, he told me about. We went down in the basement where they all where hanging out. We walked in, and Steve went around the room introducing me to everyone. We sat down and joined in the conversation. After a while of talking and getting to know a little about some of them, it seemed like they were all down to earth. I felt comfortable with them. Most of us were about the same age, and was interested in the same things, mostly music.

Dreams Lost and Found

I said to myself, here's a chance to get my music career going again. Sitting there rapping with these three guys, and two young ladies, reminded me of my old group back in Philly. I thought about my homeboy Earl in California, who called me stupid for getting married years ago, and how that was the last time I spoke to him.

We all were reminiscing about some of the music we played in our old groups. Steve broke out some old albums that took us way back, Grand funk, Jimmy Hendrix, Chicago, Earth Wind and Fire. Then the weed came out, they were already drinking beer and wine, it didn't brother me, because we all were having a good time. Later Steve's wife and her girl friends came downstairs. They brought more wine and "Rock" with them. They started lighting it up and passing it around the room. As it came closer to me, I acted like I was so involved in my conversation that I didn't notice it, so it went on to the next person. When it came back around Steve and one of the young lady's were watching. The young lady said, "come on man" you can't break the circle. I said, "no man I got a cold, I don't want everybody to catch it." They all laughed, Steve's wife said, "man you ain't got no cold, go ahead." I played it off like I was joking. I was having a good time up until then. I had never done that before, but I didn't want to look like a square in front of everyone. Steve and his wife both knew that I had never smoked "Rock" before, but

41

Morris Bussie Jr.

didn't say anything to anyone to give me away. Now when I think about it, if they were any friends of mine, they would had told everyone that I didn't do rock. As for me, instead of worrying about what people thought about me, I should have said, no thank you, I don't smoke!!"

They passed it to me, I put it to my mouth, and everyone else was involved in conversation again and wasn't paying to much attention to what I was doing. Steve's wife lit the lighter then bent over and whispered in my ear, when I put the fire to it, "pull very slowly." I glanced over at Steve before I pulled the smoke into my lungs he was looking as if he was waiting for his winning lottery numbers to be called. When the fire hit the rock and then melted down as I was pulling slowly, my ears began to ring. All of my senses came to life and I didn't have a care in the world. I could hear things that I never heard before. When I finally released the smoke from my lungs, I looked up to see Steve and his wife looking at me like proud parents watching their child take his first steps, it was like being in a whole new world.

One year earlier when I first heard about rock, people used to say all it takes is one hit to get you hooked. I didn't believe it. I said there is nothing that powerful enough to take only one time and be hooked. Well, I was wrong, and unfortunately for almost one year after that I would live in a nightmare. My whole lifestyle had changed because of one

Dreams Lost and Found

bad choice, there had been other bad choices that I made, but this was by far the worst. From that day on, I would spend a lot of time at Steve's house, after work, sometime before work, lunchtime, and on the weekends. I began to spend more time away from my family and my sons. When they would ask me why I spent so much time away from home, I told them that I was working, but children are not stupid.

Although my life was preoccupied with getting high, I always tried to maintain my appearance. "Some things you learn: never leaves you. Sometimes when I got so high, I would remember what Steve Crowder's father, back in Philly told me, "son first you have to look like somebody." It always brought me back to earth. I never would have imagined in a million years that I would be smoking "Rock." This was not the life I wanted to live.

In a few short months I had jump from the frying pan to the fire. Everyday all I could think about was trying to get that same feeling that I got the first time I tried it. That's why they say, if you take one hit "forget it," the rest of your life is spent trying to duplicate that same feeling. Every area of my life started to suffer. Here I was in my thirties a father and a husband, what was I thinking? It got so bad, that if I didn't go home on Friday with my pay check I wouldn't make it at all. What happened to the guy that had dreams of

43

Morris Bussie Jr.

being a great musician, the guy who wanted to open his on business? Everything was falling apart.

One night Steve took me to a Notorious part of South West Washington D.C. to pick up a package. It was one of the worst neighborhoods in Washington. He was somewhat of a celebrity on the street and everybody knew him. We went to a house that was the main suppliers for the area. When we walked in, there were armed guards on the door and look outs on the streets, but Steve had no problems getting us in. I was totally shocked. It wasn't the type of place that I wanted to be. That night I really started realizing that I needed to make a change in my life for myself and my family. But change wouldn't come easy.

Before I could stop completely, I went through even more. One Friday night after spending everything I had in my pocket on the first really bad binge I ever had, I decided to give the drug man my new custom Toyota Celica for collateral. I never saw him or my car again. I don't know how I did it, but up to this point I kept my problems a secret from my family. I always thought that I could stop before anyone found out, but when you come home two days later without your car and no money, you had better come clean and ask somebody for help.

Dreams Lost and Found

After talking it over with my wife and finding help, I check myself into a Rehab Hospital for thirty days. I was in Rehab with other people that were recovering from a nightmare of their own. I heard stories that made mine sound like a day at Disney Land. Some people lost everything, their homes, jobs, and family members had left them. Other people contracted aids, herpies, and many of them couldn't even go back home.

After getting out of Rehab, there was something I learned about most people that turned to drugs, somewhere along the line they were disappointed or hurt about how their life became and they lost their will to keep on trying to make it better. Most of them are very intelligent, maybe to smart for their own good.

I learned a lot about myself in thirty days. For example I need a challenge in my life, a dream, and something to make me feel productive. All the dreams I had in the past were all goals that I knew I could achieve. One night in a group meeting, the counselor asked me, what were some of the goals that I wanted to achieve before I was distracted by drugs? I shared my feeling and my disappointments as to why I didn't go to L. A. when I was nineteen, or open the Formal Wear shop when I had the opportunity. He knew immediately what type of person I was. He listened to me whine, complain, and blame other people for talking

Morris Bussie Jr.

me out of following my dreams. When I finished, he said very calmly, "do you know what you are?" You are a people pleaser. No one can stop you from following your dreams. Your whole life has been spent making everyone else happy. Everyone that has accomplished great things in their lives had to be committed and focus.

It is easy to make excuses, but the real reward is in following the dream to its completion. My mother used to tell me, "son there's a reason for everything," Maybe I had to go through that bad time in my life in order to understand that you can go as far as your mind and your will can take you. I was fortunate to make it through the drug situation, and still be in good health, and to not be in jail or dead. I was thankful for what I learned about myself while being in Rehab. Now I had a new outlook on life. I understood what the counselor told me that night in the meeting. Now it was up to me to make the changes in my life, so that I could fulfill the new dreams that would come.

"Life Changing Experience"

The day I left Rehab, there was no fanfare, no band, no one throwing confetti. It didn't matter because the way I felt that day, I hadn't felt in many years. My whole life was beginning again. I walked out of that building with a renewed energy and a will to live the life that I was meant to live. On the way home that day, I felt a little melancholy, because I knew what I had taken my family through. I knew that it would take a while to regain their trust and I was prepared to do what ever it took. My children were happy to see me, but I had to prove myself no matter what. Although I had gone through one of the worst times in my life, I began to believe in myself again and to love the person that I was capable of being. Back in Philly we had a saying "in order to be your best you

Morris Bussie Jr.

had to be at rest." Everything happens for a reason. I was a positive person again. I remember when I was a young boy back in Philly, my mother used to say "son things happen for a reason." Now I know what she was saying.

It was time to continue where I left off, I wasn't sure exactly how to do that, so I prayed and asked God to show me what to do. It wasn't easy, after being away from home for so long, to come back and act as if I had it all together. I had to humble myself and be patient. I couldn't afford to make any bad decisions. The first thing I needed to do was find a job. That was never a problem for me, because God has blessed me with an outgoing personality. Within a week, I found a job at a uniform shop in downtown Washington as a salesman/tailor. The job only paid two-hundred and fifty dollars a week, but I was thankful to have it. It didn't take long to learn about the business, but it was much different from the other job I had as a tailor. The name of the shop was Muscatellos. We supplied uniforms for the police department, security companies, and metro bus and rail. Mr. Muscatellos started the business back in the early sixty's. He retired in the mid 80s and sold the business to Bob and Gege Morgan who were some of the nicest people I have ever met. The manager of the shop was Phil Curiton, we became the best of friends.

Dreams Lost and Found

I learned all about the uniform business from Phil. Everyday he would take time to teach me something about the different manufactures that we used, or how to place an order for a particular item. Phil took me under his wings, and I was willing to learn all I could. He reminded me of the old heads back in Philadelphia, when they would talk to me about being successful and to always be willing to learn.

My life was beginning to take shape again. Everyday I looked forward to going to work. Phil and I had the same outgoing personality. We would do anything for our customers to make them happy. After about six months of seeing the same customers, I began to learn their needs. When they would come into the store, we had so much inventories in one building that it would take a year to remember where all of it was, but it only took me a few months. Bob and Gege were so impressed to see how fast I learned where everything was, they gave me a raise after three months. Years ago back in Philly I over heard Mr. Crowder telling one of his sons, after he came home from work complaining about something that happened, he said "you don't have to break your back for anyone just do your job the best you can and when the time comes it will payoff. "When I went to work at Muscatellos I wanted to show them that I was a good and competent worker, and it paid off. After the ruff year I had, I wanted nothing more than to prove that it could happen to anyone.

49

Morris Bussie Jr.

But it's up to the individual what happens next. You can use that experience to make your life better or stay where you are and die a slow death. When I spent a month in Rehab, everyday I would focus on my life after I got out, because I knew if I went back to Rehab it would be harder to recover the next time. One thing I found out was, you have to stay around the right people. I was so determined to be the best person that I could be, that anyone who I thought was getting high, I wanted no part of them. God puts the right people in your life when you do the right things. Everyday was a new opportunity for me to do the right thing. After being on the job for eight months, my wife and I decided to move from Oxon Hill M.D. because it was to close to South West Washington where I used to hang out with Steve. I didn't want to be anywhere around those old memories.

We moved to Upper Marlboro, Maryland which was about thirty minutes from Washington D.C. It was the perfect area for our children. The school system was much better than the one we left, and our sons received better grades. The house had five bedrooms, two and a half bathrooms, a large family room, fire place and it was on a corner lot with room for four cars. It felt like we were in a whole different city, and it was all worth it. Our children were happy to be away from so many negative influences. I was quit surprised to hear them talk about how much they disliked our old

Dreams Lost and Found

neighborhood. After we talked about it, I encouraged them to always speak their mind and tell us what they were feeling. I knew I had to spend more time talking with them, because I didn't want them to get hung up in the same things that I did. My wife still had them in church every Friday night and Sunday morning so they had a good foundation.

For me, work was important. My job was o.k., but it wasn't what I wanted to do for the rest of my life. So I began to pray and believe that I would find a job that would allow me to meet people that could help me in my true calling.

One day a customer of mine came into the store, I noticed that he always ordered a dark suit. He was always in a good mood, very cheerful and upbeat. No matter how busy I was when he came in, he would wait until I was finished with my other customers. I had built up my own clientele and he was one of them. What I liked about working with the public is that when you build a personal relationship, you become a part of their family. After being at Muscatellos for a year, I had just as many steady customers as Phil did. Bob and Gege, the owners of the business, were impressed with my work ethic and my out going personality.

After waiting for about ten minutes, I was ready to take care of "Mr. Guy." We began to talk as usual about what ever the hot topic was for that week. I knew that he was there to

51

Morris Bussie Jr.

get a dark suit, so as we talked, I walked him over to where the suits were. This man was a wealth of knowledge!! He had been all over the country, and had some great stories about some of the people he worked for. As I stood listening to him, I couldn't help but to ask what he did. In my mind, I thought that he was a mortician because he always bought dark suits. When I asked him, he said, "I'm a Chauffeur, didn't you know? No! I said. Yes, he said. I have been a Chauffeur for twenty one years. It's the best job I ever had. We talked for about thirty minutes. He shared some of his experiences with me. Some were funny and some were unbelievable. Suddenly he stopped talking and said, "You know you would make a great Chauffeur." I said, "You have got to be kidding" I don't know the first thing about it. Then I thought to myself about what Mr. Crowder would say. "Always keep an open mind and always be willing to try something new." So I asked Mr. Guy to tell me more about being a Chauffer. He gave me his card and said, "When you are ready to try it, give me a call and I'll put you in contact with a company. I was so excited about having an opportunity to drive around the city in a big black shinny car, that I went home and talked to my wife about it, but she didn't share the same excitement.

I called my sister Laura, who was also living in Washington now. We met the next day for lunch and I told her all about

Dreams Lost and Found

it. She encouraged me to try it, and give it my best. I called Mr. Guy two days later and said o.k. Mr. Guy I'm going to give it a shot." He was even more excited than I was. He said, "Morris take my word for it, you are going to be great at it." This was a man who saw something in me, and he was willing to put his name on the line for me.

Mr. Guy gave me the name of a company in Virginia. The company was Elite Limousine. I called the next day to set up an interview for that next Monday. I put on my best Navy blue suit, with a crisp white shirt. My shoes were as black and as shinny as I could get them. What I learned in Philly many years ago never left me, "first you have to look like somebody." I could tell I made an impression on the owner of the company right away. When I walked in his office, the first thing he said was nice suit. I learned that looking important was the first step to making a lasting impression. Even if I had never driven anyone professionally before, I had to know something about the Business.

So before I went on the interview, I did my homework. Besides getting some tips from Mr. Guy, if I saw a Chauffeur on the street I would ask him about how to handle different situations. Some of what they said made sense and some didn't. I came to the conclusion that being a good Chauffeur was just good common sense. The interview was going well. He asked me have I ever driven anybody before. At first I

Morris Bussie Jr.

was tempted to say yes, but I knew that Mr. Guy was a good friend of his so I had to be honest. When I told him no, he said well, I believe your going to do just fine. I hesitated for a second, then said, "you mean I have the job?" "Yes you do" he said. Mr. Guy thinks you'll be good at it. And I think he's right. He asked me how well I knew the city and if I could read a map, I told him it would be no problem.

I went home after the interview feeling like I had hit the lottery and then I went to work. The next day I gave Bob and Gege my one week notice. They were not happy to hear that I was leaving and even offered to give me more money. The offer was tempting but sometimes it's not the money, it's the satisfaction of doing something that makes you feel alive. My friend Phil was disappointed, but he understood that I wanted more out of life.

When the following Monday came, I was so excited to start my new career. On the way to pick up the car from the office in Virginia, I began to get a little nervous thinking of all the possibilities of what could happen on my first day. When I arrived at the office, Jeff the owner, was outside by the car waiting for me. I guess he wanted to see if I would be on time, after all that's what the whole business is about. When I got out of the car, he gave me an inspection to see if I was dressed properly. If he was trying to find flaws in the way I dressed that would not be the area. As we went over

Dreams Lost and Found

some things about the car he, asked me "what would be the first thing I would do when I arrived to pick up a passenger? Because I had never done it before, I let my common sense take over. I said first, I would park where they could see me. Then as they approached the car, I would introduce myself as their Chauffeur, then put their lugged in the trunk, and make sure they were comfortably seated in the back seat. He looked at me and said, that's good when you are picking them up at their home, but how would they know that the car is for them if you're in front of our office building? I though for a minute, but couldn't come up with an answer. I felt so stupid when he said, you have to have a sign in your window. That one simple detail bothered me for the rest of the day. I hated not knowing the answers to a simple problem.

As we finished going over some details, he gave me my work orders for that day. He put his hand on my shoulder and said, "just relax and stay loose" and you'll be fine. Just remember if you're nervous the passenger will know it. Always make sure you know where you are going before hand and if there is a problems, call me right away. As my day got started, I said a prayer and asked God to help me make it through. I arrived at the first pick up location and I remembered what Jeff said to me, "if you're nervous the passenger will know it." So not to appear nervous, I imagined myself there to pick up

55

Morris Bussie Jr.

a friend, but the only difference was, I couldn't talk to them unless they talked to me.

As I waited for the passenger to come out of the house, the thought ran across my mind, once again that first impression is the lasting one. The door to the house opened and out came the passenger. I stepped out of the car and walked up to meet her at the door. My God given personality took over. I introduced myself as her chauffeur and picked up her luggage. She was a nice lady that seemed more nervous than I was about going over seas for a business trip. After she was comfortably in the back seat, I put her luggage in the trunk. We started out for the airport. She asked me if traffic would be bad. It was about nine o'clock Monday morning and we were going from Northwest Washington to Dulles Airport, so I knew that we would run into a little traffic. So I said, "ma'am I think we might run into a little but it won't be bad." From that first day, I learned that being a good Chauffeur is like being a concierge. You have to be prepared to answer the small everyday questions. For example what's the temperature today or is it going to rain today? Some passengers even want to know what the top story in the news is for that day. So I made it a habit to get a newspaper every morning.

After my first passenger arrived safely at the airport, I called Jeff to let him know. He asked if I had any problems, I said no. Everything went well. I had two other passengers

Dreams Lost and Found

that day, and by the last one I knew that this was something I could really be great at. This job was all about making people feel comfortable while they are in your presence and getting them safely to their destination.

The following next day Tuesday, it was a whole new experience Jeff had put me with one of his more difficult clients. This man had a reputation for being rude with the Chauffeurs I guess Jeff wanted to see how I would handle myself in a tough situation. Over the years I had become a good judge of character. So when I arrived to pick this passenger up, I could tell right away that I was in for trouble. I got to his house fifteen minutes early and was waiting for him to come out, when I saw the front door open. I got out of the car and went to meet him to get his luggage. I introduced myself and grabbed the bags. He didn't say a word at first, I thought to myself, how rude. When I walked him back to the car and opened the door for him, he said, just put the bags in the trunk and let's go. It took everything in my power to continue to be a gentleman. I put the luggage in the trunk and closed it down firmly. When I got in the car, I looked in the rear view mirror I noticed his expression had changed. I guess from the way I put the trunk down he knew that I wasn't the one. I was always taught that you should treat people like you want to be treated, so if he

Morris Bussie Jr.

wanted nasty that's what I would give him, but in a way that was professional.

As we started out for the airport, there was stone silence. He noticed that I had two newspapers, the Washington Post and the Wall Street Journal. Suddenly he said, do you get those papers every morning? Yes, I said in a strong stern voice. Then he asked me if I was a new driver? "Yes" Again I said. He pulled the Wall Street Journal out of the back of the seat and began to read it. As we got closer to the Airport, he asked me what was my name? After I told him my name he said, "Morris you're a very good driver, and for the rest of the trip to the Airport we talked. He told me that he had some bad experiences with drivers before, so to him all drivers were the same. I said, well I'm sorry to hear that you had some unpleasant memories, but I happen to enjoy what I do and that makes a difference. He said, "I can tell because you even dress better than most drivers. From that point on every time he needed to be picked up, he would request me to come. Jeff could not believe it, he said to me, "I don't know what you did to this guy but he thinks you are great.

After all I have been through, and the year that I almost lost it. It brings me to this point in my life. I had something to offer the world and now it was time to find those lost dreams and move on.

Dreams Lost and Found

God has blessed me with a gift and it was time to take it to the world I was down and confused my dreams were lost. Now it was time to let my light shine.

"My Wildest Experience as a Chauffeur"

In early 1995, I had been working for Elite Limousine for a few months and quickly became good at it. Just as Mr. Guy predicted, one day Jeff called me into his office and said to me, "Morris I have met some of the Washington Redskin players and told them about the business." They will be calling, and I want you to drive them. "No problem" I said. Before Jeff met the Redskins, we didn't have many celebrity passengers. As a matter of fact, we didn't have any at all. The following Friday night, Jeff called me and said he needed me to meet Chris Mims, the Skins defensive line backer at the

Morris Bussie Jr.

Airport and take him to his apartment in Sterling VA. I said no problem, I will be there.

That year I wasn't following the Skins as a true fan should, so I wasn't sure what he looked like. I arrived at the Airport and made out a sign reading "Mims." While standing at the gate holding up the sign, and waiting to see a big dude with a lot of people around him, asking for his autograph. A young Lady walked up to me and said, "Hi I'm ready to go," I laughed and said "ok let's go."

As I continued to stand there holding the sign she said, "Chris sent you to pick me up right?" I was so embarrassed to find out that I wasn't picking up Chris himself but one of his lady friends. On the way out to the car, I explained to her that sometimes when I'm at the airport holding up a sign, some people walk up to me and jokingly say, that's me I'm ready. That's why I thought that you were joking around, I'm sorry. She laughed and began to tell me that she had done it before also. As we were headed to Chris's apartment, she asked me if I knew Chris, I said no, I have never met him. She said he is o.k. you'll see.

When I got her to Chris's house, she called him to let him know that we were outside. When he came out, I couldn't believe how big the guy was. As I got out of the car, he walked over to meet us and when I opened her door, she

Dreams Lost and Found

jumped out and ran over to him and gave him a big hug. I could tell right away that Chris was a good guy from the way he carried himself. After he gave his friend a hug, he walked over to me and shook my hand. He gave me a crisp one hundred dollar bill and said, "man, I appreciate you picking up my girl." "Mr. Mims, it was my pleasure I said. He said please call me Chris, and asked me for my business card. After I grabbed the luggage out of the trunk and walked up to his door I said, o.k. Chris is there anything else I can do for you. He said no, but I'll need you on Sunday afternoon to take my friend back to the Airport. No problem, I said, "I'll be here.

Later that night after I got home Jeff called to ask how things went with Chris? Everything went great. He's a good dude I said. Jeff said, "this could be the start of a good relationship between us and the Redskins, but it all depends on how you handle it. I said oh well if you leave it up to me, the Redskins will call on us when ever they need a car, I'll be there. For the few weeks I had to show Jeff that I was a man of my word. Chris was calling us two or three times a week sometimes if not for himself, then for one of his home boys.

One Friday night, we got a call from Chris, he wanted me to pick him up from his apartment in Sterling VA. When I got there, it was him and another Redskin's players, whom I didn't know, but this guy had the perfect body. He stood

63

about six five, and had massive arms, his waist was maybe a thirty-four, his chest and abdomen was perfectly cut. I didn't think that it was possible for me to be jealous of anybody, but this was one time I felt maybe a little inadequate.

As the three of us were standing on the outside of the Limo, Chris said, "Morris have you ever heard of a club in D.C. called the Republic Garden?" I said, man, that's probably the hottest club in Washington right now." He said, "cool, that's where we want to go tonight." I opened up the doors of the Limo so they could get in. Chris said to his home boy, what is she doing? Up until this time, I thought it was just Chris and his homeboy. As Chris started to walk back to his apartment, the door opened and out came the most beautiful woman that I have ever seen. I thought to myself, there is no way that she is with these guys. Then I remembered that these guys play for the NFL. She closed the door to Chris's apartment and walks toward the Limo. I couldn't help but to think to myself this is going to be an interesting evening.

After getting everyone in the Limo, we started driving towards D.C. The young lady had never been to Washington before and she wanted to see a little bit of the city, so on the way to the club, I drove by some of the Monuments, like the Jefferson Memorial, Washington Monument, and the White House. After the short tour, we headed for the club. When

Dreams Lost and Found

we got to 14th & U Street there were so many people on the street that the police had to close the block off. Chris said, "Morris can you get us through?" I'm going to try I said. I drove up to the police barricade and got out, walked over to the officer and said, "I have a couple of Redskin players that are supposed to make an appearance here at the club tonight and sign some autographs." The officer looked at me and said, "man, you better not be lying to me." And he walked over to the Limo. He knocked on the rear window, and Chris put the window down, immediately the officer knew who he was. Chris said, "hey officer we are just trying to get to the club. The officer said, "no problem." Then turned back to me and said you can park right in front of the door.

When I got back in the Limo Chris said, "Morris you are the man." That night I found out just what being a celebrity means. The officer removed the barricade and waved me through. When I pulled up in front of the club, everybody that was standing in line was watching to see who was going to get out of the Limo. When I stepped out and walked back to the right side passenger door to open it, one of the bouncers from the club walked over to me and asked me, "Do you have a V.I.P. in the car?" I whispered to him yes, it's a couple of Redskin players, he said, o.k. Ask them if they wanted to use the rear entrance? I opened the door just a little and asked Chris if he wanted to go through the front or

Morris Bussie Jr.

the rear entrance? Chris said, "No we will use the front door. When I opened the door and let them out, everyone in line and on the street started cheering.

The women were going crazy. Everybody rushed for autographs. Chris, his girlfriend, and teams mate, kept moving toward the club. After they got inside, I stayed outside with the Limo and talked to some people that were still standing in line. After about three hours, Chris and his lady friend came out. They had been drinking heavily so they were feeling good. Chris and his young lady walked over to the Limo. He asked me if I had seen Kirk, his homeboy, I said no I have not seen him. Just then Kirk walks out of the club with three women hanging on his arm. Chris turned to me laughed, and said, "you see Morris that's why I can't take him anywhere.

Kirk was the perfect specimen of a man. Most of the men at the club that night were checking him out, some were jealous, and some wanted to know how long it took for him to get like that. All of the women just wanted to feel his arms and abs. Chris called Kirk over to the Limo, Kirk turned to the women that were hanging on to him and said I'll be right back. Kirk walked up to Chris with a big smile on his face. Chris asked him if he was ready to go? Kirk said, "O.K. man just give me ten more minutes," and walked back over to the three women he had waiting. Chris and his lady

Dreams Lost and Found

friend got into the Limo. I was still parked in front of the club. People were coming over to the Limo asking Chris for his autograph, while we were sitting there waiting for Kirk to come back, so that we could head back to Sterling V.A. Fifteen minutes had pasted Chris and his lady friend were sitting in the back of the Limo talking. Then it got quiet Chris reached up to the controls over his head and pushed the button to close the partition.

It was already after 1 a.m. and a half hour had gone by since Kirk told us that he would be back. At this point I thought to myself, I might as well get comfortable, so I laid my seat back as far as it would go. Then Chris voice came over the intercom and said, "Morris go across the street and park in the alley, O.K. no problem I said. I went around the block and came back up through the alley so I could see Kirk when he came out.

I parked the Limo at the edge of the alley and got out to stretch my legs. After five minutes, I got back into the Limo and said to myself this is turning out to be a long night. I put my head back and began to get comfortable again I closed my eyes and dosed off. Suddenly I was awakened by the Limo shaking and bouncing around. It scared me at first, because I thought someone might be trying to rob Chris after they saw us pull into the alley. But after looking in both of the side mirrors before getting out of the Limo to investigate, I

Morris Bussie Jr.

didn't see neither of the doors open. So I called out to Chris and I didn't get an answer, by this time the Limo was really bouncing so I decided to see what was going on. I reached up to the controls and put the partition down and got the surprise of my life. Fortunately they didn't notice. When I put the partition down to investigate why the Limo was bouncing around, they had the rear speaker system blasting, so they couldn't hear the partition go down. I don't think they were paying to much attention to anything else.

This was the first experience I ever had like this so, I didn't know exactly how to handle it. I got out of the car and walked around for a few minutes. As I'm standing on the outside of the Limo, people were walking by and notice that the Limo was moving. They look at me, and look at the Limo, and said, "Oh boy," somebody having a good time. This went on for about fifteen minutes. Then Chris calls out, "Morris lets go."

I got back into the car and pushed the intercom button and said, "Chris what about Kirk?" Chris responded, "don't worry about Kirk he'll be alright. I put the Limo in drive and began to head back to Stealing V.A., which is about a fifty minutes drive. As I got on fourteen street, headed towards the G.W. parkway, Chris and his lady friend were still getting busy. As I pulled up to each traffic light, people would pull up next to the Limo and look over at me as if they knew what

Dreams Lost and Found

was going on in the back. When I finally got to the George Washington Parkway, I had a hard time controlling the Limo because of the bouncing. It had been thirty minutes since they started and they were still going strong. I wanted to get to Chris house as soon as I could so instead of going the speed limit I was going about 75 miles an hour. This made it even harder to control a car that was almost the size of a bus.

At one point, they were going at it so hard that it felt like I was on a roller coaster. It took exactly fifty minutes to get to Chris house. When I pulled up in front of his apartment, they didn't notice until I cut the Limo off. The stereo stopped, the light went off, and Chris said, "Oh good job Morris we are here." They took a couple of minutes to get themselves together. I waited a couple of minutes before I walked to the rear of the Limo to let them out. They got out of the Limo with a big smile on their faces.

Chris turned to me and said, "Morris tonight was fun, let's do it again." Then he handed me two hundred dollar bills. After they went into Chris's apartment, I had to sit there for a few minutes to get myself together. I couldn't believe what just happened. I had never experienced anything like that before but this was only the beginning.

Morris Bussie Jr.

The second wildest experience was three months after becoming a Chauffeur. I quickly learned that this business brings out the real side of peoples personalities. One hot June Saturday evening, I was scheduled to pick up a group of young white females for a bachelorette party. I picked them up at nine p.m. from Reston V.A. When I arrived to pick up the young ladies, they all were very professional and polite. It appeared that most of them were from well to do families and were college educated. I said that because they had every part of their evening planed and they knew exactly what they wanted to do.

One young lady who was the spokeswoman, for the group asked me to take them to Adams Morgan, which was a trendy part of Washington D.C. As we headed to D.C., the young ladies were talking about the upcoming wedding the next day. I remember thinking to myself, "boy these chicks don't know how to have a good time, they are to booshy." As we got closer to Adams Morgan, the spokeswoman for the group came up to the partition in the Limo and said, "driver, we want to go to "Felix first so we can get something to eat." I said, "sure no problem." Felix is a trendy restaurant on 18Th street in Adams Morgan that has live Jazz and a laid back atmosphere. When I pulled up to "Felix" I had to double park in order to let the ladies out.

Dreams Lost and Found

As I walked to the back of the Limo, I could hear one of the young ladies say, "that's a fine black man, I'm going to see what's up with him later." When I reached the rear passenger door and opened it to let them out, they all got out smiling, so I didn't know which one said it. Before they went into the restaurant, I made sure that I gave Susan the cell phone number in case I had to park in the next block.

They stayed in the restaurant about an hour and a half. When they came out of the restaurant Susan called for me to pull the car down and pick them up. As I pulled down in front of Felix's, it seemed like I was seeing a whole new set of women. I double parked in front of the restaurant and put my flashers on. Saturday Night is one of the busiest nights in Adams Morgan. It is never an easy time trying to find a place to park as especially for a Limo. When I stepped out of the car, the young ladies were much more alive and ready to party.

They were saying things like "hay Morris, what's happening sweetheart." Dude, you got some big hands, is it true what they say about men with big hands? I could tell that it was going to be a night to remember. As I was helping the ladies in the Limo, one at a time, I felt one of the ladies up close behind me, when I turned around she said, "I'm sorry, I didn't realize that I was leaning on you." The night was young and we had only made one of their scheduled three stops. If this

Morris Bussie Jr.

is how they were after the first stop, I could imagine what the rest of the night would be like.

The next stop was a club called Heaven and Hell it was also in Adams Morgan. The club was at the opposite end of 18Th Street. I told the ladies that I would have to circle the block. They said it would be O.K., because they had to handle some business before they were ready to go inside. Susan, the spokeswoman of the group, asked if I would put the partition up, I said sure, no problem. When I got to the front of the club, they asked me to circle one more time, I said O.K. Half way down the street it was evident why they wanted the partition up.

They fired up some weed that was so strong that it made me light headed. At the time I didn't know what to say, because Jeff never said to me that the passengers couldn't smoke weed in the Limo. So I thought to myself what should I do at this point. I waited until we got back around in front of the club. As I was letting the ladies out of the Limo, I could tell that smoking weed was new to one of them. It was a sight that I have never seen before. First she would throw up then she would laugh like crazy, then throw up again. All of the other young ladies thought that it was the funniest thing they ever saw.

Dreams Lost and Found

As the other ladies went inside, Susan and the young lady that was sick one second and laughing the next, stayed behind until she could get herself together. I pulled Susan to the side and said something like "you know I could get into a lot of trouble if I get stopped by the police and you all are smoking in the Limo?" Susan said, "O.K. Morris I'm sorry, it will not happen again." Thank you I said, then she put her arms around me and hugged me for a long time. When she let go, she said, "that felt good."

I knew it was the alcohol and the weed talking, because if she saw me on the street any other day, she wouldn't give me a second look. After that, she turned back to the other young lady whose name was Alice, and said, "are you ready to go in now?" Alice looked up and said, "I think I'll stay in the Limo for awhile. Susan turned to me and asked if it would be o.k. I said "it's o.k. I'll keep her company." Susan went into the club and I closed the door of the Limo, and got in behind the wheel on the driver side.

After getting in, Alice said, "Morris why don't you come back here and sit with me for awhile? I said, "I had better stay up in the front in case I have to move the Limo." She said, I'll come up here, I won't bite. As she moved from the rear seat to the seat right behind the driver's seat, it seemed to me that Alice was feeling much better, because she wanted to talk all of a sudden. I turned to her and asked how was

Morris Bussie Jr.

she feeling? She said, I'm feeling much better, then she asked me if I was married? Yes I said. We talked for an hour. She asked about everything such as where I was from and If I had any children? When she asked me how old I was, she thought that I was lying when I told her my age, and asked to see my driver's license.

An hour and a half had gone by when two of the young ladies came out to the Limo to check on Alice. When they got in the Limo, I could tell that they were smashed one of the ladies said to Alice, what have ya'll been doing in here, because it smells like sex? Then they all started laughing. Alice said, "why did you come back to the Limo I'm trying to get some. I couldn't believe that these were the same ladies I had picked up four hours earlier.

It's a fact, that when people drink you find out exactly who they are. As we all were sitting there talking about sex, they were asking me questions about why black men are bigger, and why is it that when white women go black they don't go back? I must admit, I was beginning to get aroused. But I think that was the plan of the ladies from the beginning. They were horny and they wanted me to be horny to. Susan came back to the Limo and asked the ladies to come back in the club for a toast to the bride.

Dreams Lost and Found

I was relieved, and was able to regain my composure they stayed in the club until one thirty a.m. When they finally came out, some of them could barely walk. I was totally surprised!! These couldn't be the same sophisticated, highly intelligent women that I picked up six hours earlier. Most of the women didn't even want to look in my face earlier, but now they were all happy to see me, and wanted to give me a hug. It took about thirty minutes to get them all in the car, and when we did, one young lady filled up the champagne glasses with vomit. When I first picked up these ladies, I thought to myself this is going to be a boring evening, but as it turned out, it was an evening to remember. As we headed back to Reston Virginia, where I picked them up, they began to break out gifts for the young lady that was getting married. Susan called out to me and said, "Morris, I'm going to put the partition up because we have some things for the bride that you can't see. I said, "no problem."

As I reached rout 66, they had gotten so rowdy that people driving next to us were looking and pointing. I could hear them saying things like, oh my God look at the size of that thing. Go ahead see if you can us it. At first I thought maybe they were talking about underwear or something else to wear. But then all a sudden the partition came down and one young lady whose name I found out later was Jennifer, comes popping threw with a sex toy in her hand. Everyone

Morris Bussie Jr.

in the rear of the Limo was laughing like crazy. I wasn't paying to much attention because I was driving.

The laughing was going on for almost two or three minutes without anybody saying anything so I decided to turn around to see what was going on. As I turned around, I saw a huge sex toy next to my face. All the ladies were laughing and going crazy. Then one of the ladies said, "hey Morris I bet yours is bigger than that!! At this point I'm totally speechless. I knew bachelor parties were wild, but this was the first time I had ever experienced women as wild as that.

At 2:45 a.m. we were back in Reston VA, where I had picked them up. The next job was getting them out of the Limo. One young lady had fallen asleep and no one could keep her awake. She would wake up for a second, mumble something then fall right back to sleep. I pulled into the circular driveway, put the Limo in park, then got out and walked to the rear doors, opened the door and got an eye full. One of the young ladies had pulled her skirt all the way up to her waist and was holding her underwear in her hand. No one else seemed to notice this but me. She stumbled out of the Limo, threw her arms around me with her skirt still up to her waist and said, "Morris my man what's happing? Now here I am a black male in an affluent neighborhood in Reston

Dreams Lost and Found

VA, with a white woman with her skirt up around her waist giving me a hug at 2:45 a.m. It was not a good thing.

I couldn't wait to get those ladies out of the Limo, so that I could go home. Susan was still trying to wake the other young lady up that had fallen asleep, as the others began to get out slowly. I found out why the young lady had her skirt up to her waist with he underwear in her hand. As I was helping everyone out of the Limo, she had knelt down behind the car to urinate. I was amazed because again no one else seemed to notice her action but me.

These ladies were so smashed that they didn't realize what they were doing. For most of them, it was probably there first time drinking. They finally were able to wake the young lady up. Just before we could get her out of the Limo, she threw up all over the carpet. It was a nightmare. Susan's mother heard the ladies from inside the house and came out. I could tell by the look on her face that she had never seen these women act like this before.

Susan was intoxicated also, but was not as drunk as the rest of them, so she was able to help get the others in the house. She asked me to wait until she came back out, I said O.K. Meanwhile I started cleaning out the Limo. It was now 3.10 a.m. I thought that it would be a good idea to call Jeff the owner of the company, just to let him know what

Morris Bussie Jr.

was going on. It didn't matter to me what time it was, I just wanted him to know what happen inside the Limo, so I wouldn't get the rap for the damage that was done. When I got Jeff on the phone, I let him know that I had a night from hell. He asked, what happened? I told him I would have to tell him later, but for right now, the Limo is trashed and one of the ladies threw up all over the carpet.

Just then Susan came back out of the house and walked over to where I was standing. It appeared that she and her mother had an argument. I asked if everything was o.k. and if there was anything that I could do? She laughed and said yes, let's go get a room. She didn't seem to care who I was talking to on the phone at the time, so I played it off and continued to talk to Jeff, but Jeff heard every word she said. He told me to inform her that she would be charged one hundred and fifty dollars for the cleaning of the carpet, and two Champagne glasses that had gotten broken. When I got off the phone with Jeff, I explained to Susan that her credit card would be charged for the cleaning of the Limo. She said she understands and it would be ok. She would just get all the ladies to chip in and pay her back.

After taking care of the business changes, she grabbed my hand and put a wad of bills in it, and said this is for you then gave me a big hug and said I have your card I'm going to call you sometimes. I took the bills and put them in my pocket

Dreams Lost and Found

without looking to see how much it was. Susan turned around, waved goodbye then went inside the house.

My night wasn't over yet. There was still the matter of getting the rear of the Limo clean. On the way back to Jeff to drop off the Limo, and pick up my car I stopped into the gas station and removed the trash, and tried to clean up the vomit before it set in. Now it's 4:15 a.m. and here I am in a gas station, in a long black Limo with all the doors and windows open, cleaning up someone else vomit. My mind went back to something that my friends father told me when I was fifteen years old back in Philly. "What ever you do, be the best at it." Well, my goal when I started this job was to be one of the best, "if not the best." Unfortunately this was a part of this particular job.

After ten minutes of cleaning, I decided that it was time to find a company that had a better clientele. The next day I began my search. One thing about being a Chauffeur in Washington D.C., is that there are so many Limo Companies, that it's not hard to find work. The trick is finding the company with a good clientele. I stayed with Jeff for the next two weeks. During that time as I would see other Chauffeurs on the street I would ask them questions about the companies they worked for in order to get a feel of the clientele they had and how well they treated their Chauffeurs. When I made my mind up to leave Jeff's company, he wasn't very happy,

79

Morris Bussie Jr.

but he understood. We said our good bys and promised to stay in touch.

"Never stay in a situation when you know you can do better," somewhere else. An old head called "Sugarbear" shared that with me back in Philadelphia many years ago. He was a giant of a man that always had some wisdom to share when ever you saw him. That's how he got the name "Sugarbear" because he always had something good to say.

"Hanging with the Stars"

When I decided it was time for me to move on, I remembered a gentleman that I had met months earlier whose name was John. He worked for a company in Rockville Maryland. At the time we met, we were at Washington's National Airport waiting, to pick up passengers from the same flight. We instantly hit it off. He reminded me of my old mentor back in Philly, "Mr. Crowder. John was an older gentleman who was retired from the government, and was now working as a professional Chauffeur. He was the perfect example of what a Chauffeur was ment to be. As we stood there, talking and waiting on our flight to land, we exchanged business cards. He told me, if I ever needed help with anything or if I had a question, to give him a call.

Morris Bussie Jr.

When I made up my mind to leave Elite Limousine, John was the first person I called. I told him that I was interested in working with his company. I asked him if he could set up an interview with his boss. John said, "it would be his pleasure. He gave me his boss's office number, and told me that he would talk to him, and ask him to call me." One week later, I received a called from Johns boss, and two days after that, I started my new job. John had giving his boss such a good reference of me, that I didn't even have to go in to the office for an interview. That's what happens when you carry yourself well and people respect you. This man hired me sight unseen and on the recommendation of one of his best Chauffeurs. It's good when you can develop relationships where people can trust and believe in you and you in them.

After two weeks of working at the new company, I began to develop relationships with other drivers. Over the years, I had become a pretty good judge of character. I quickly found out who to stay away from. There was another gentleman that worked for the company that I became friends with also. He was a little younger then I but he was a serious professional. His name was Fletcher Moses, and he worked in the office. Fletcher could do everyone's job, he knew the ends and outs of the whole business, and could tell you whatever you needed to know about it.

Dreams Lost and Found

At the time I started with the company my wife and I decided to call it quits. It became very hard for me to stay focused on anything and it was beginning to show. Being a new employee on any job, you have to always be at your best. It was hard to go to work everyday with my problems at home on my mind. Fletcher and I both lived in Upper Marlboro, MD at the time, and sometimes he would give me a ride to and from home if I didn't drive that day. One day on the ride home, Fletcher asked me if everything was alright, because it seemed like I had a lot on my mind.

Usually I don't share my problems with anybody, but it was beginning to affect my work and everything else. After I talked and got it off my chest, Fletcher said, that he had gone through the same thing and not to let it get the best of me. Life goes on he said, "so get yourself together and move on." He told me just what I needed to do.

Sometimes God puts people in your life at the right time. I was trying very hard to keep things in perspective and work harder on my marriage, but it just wasn't happening. Meanwhile, I was missing work and having a hard time sleeping. I think what hurt me the most, is that my reputation for being a man of character and a person that was dependable, was in jeopardy. It was hard for me to wake up in the morning, because I usually didn't fall a sleep until after 2 a.m.

Morris Bussie Jr.

One morning after I missed a very important client, Fletcher called me and he was very angry. He said, "man, we talked about your problems, but it seems you would rather do nothing about it and let it eat you up instead of moving on. He said some other things that I would rather not share with anyone, but I think you get the picture.

That day, I learned that Fletcher was a good friend, because what he said to me, bought me out of the toughest time in my life. I moved on, and the whole world opened up to me. I thanked God for bringing people into my life to help me grow.

Unfortunately, I had to move on to anther job as well, but that's all a part of the growth process. The next company I went to was Dav-el. They had offices world wide and the clientele was top notch. After going through a mandatory training program, it didn't matter how much experience I had, I had to learn to do things the Dav-el way. They put me to work three days later, and one of the very first clients I drove was Val Kilmer. At that time, back in 1999 Val Kilmer was a household name because he had stared in movies as Wyatt Earp and Batman Returns.

Dreams Lost and Found

It was October of 1999, I walked into the Dav-el office for the first time, to start work after the three day training program. The first person I met when I walked in was a short but very cool Japanese guy, by the name of Mike Yamada. Mike was very well known in the business as one of the best. We hit it off right away, and he became my go to guy when I needed advice.

It was a Thursday night, and after a couple of a airport transfers I got a call from the office dispatch. The dispatcher joyfully told me that he was about to give me my first big celebrity. Well it was my very first day and after all of my training, I was ready for the big time. After the dispatcher

Morris Bussie Jr.

sent me the job, I carefully read the instructions, and then started out for the airport. I was so excited that I arrived at the airport one hour early. I used the time to go over my car with a fine tooth comb. One thing I quickly gained, was a reputation for having an exquisite car. No matter what the weather condition, when I pulled up to my pickup location my car was clean. Sometimes, it wouldn't stay clean because of rain or snow, but when I first got there it had to be clean. Val Kilmer flight arrived thirty minutes late. When he and his assistant arrived at the gate I was, the six foot tall one standing in a black suit, black shoes, white shirt, with a company tie and a Dav-el Lapel pin.

Usually, we would hold up a sign so that people would know that we are there to pick them up, but whenever I'm picking up a celebrity, I don't use a sign. Because for one thing, when people see a name that they recognize, they get curious and them before you know it, people are walking up to you asking questions about who you are picking up. Celebrities are recognizable. So there is no need to draw attention by holding up a sign with their name on it. I have found that if you are dressed as a professional, when you see your passengers, you walk up to them introduce yourself as their Chauffeur, and hand them a business card. They appreciate that you are sensitive to their need to be inconspicuous. Some drivers that I've seen at the airport,

Dreams Lost and Found

waiting on a celebrity, want people to know that they are picking up a celebrity. These are clearly inexperienced and unprofessional drivers and not Chauffeurs.

As Val Kilmer and his assistant walked through the security gate, they noticed me standing there. Once I made eye contact, I walked over and introduced myself as their Chauffeur. They were relieved to see me standing there. Obviously they must have had a bad experience with a Sedan service picking them up before. After I greeted them at the gate, we walked through the airport to the parking garage. On the way, passersby noticed who he was but were ether to afraid or to star struck to say everything.

Val Kilmer was the first big star I had the opportunity to drive, other than some Redskins players that I drove when I first started in the business. I was a little nervous at first, but quickly learned that celebrities are just like everyone else when it comes to being comfortable and relaxed. When celebrities are in the company of people they don't know, they study you for awhile and watch your demeanor. The more relaxed you are, the more comfortable they will be with you. It's always been my goal, to no matter what the situation stay cool and relaxed.

The next two days I was hanging out with Val Kilmer and his friend. I was taking them to their meetings, to dinner and

Morris Bussie Jr.

a little doing a little shopping. When I finally took him back to the airport to catch his flight out, he said to me Morris, whenever I come back to Washington I'm going to ask for you. I said, "Mr. Kilmer it would be my pleasure to be of service whenever you are here." As I pulled up to the airport and let them out. As I removed their luggage from the trunk, Val Kilmer and I shook hands and said our good bys.

I waited until they walked inside the terminal before I got in the car to pull off. As I was leaving the airport, I couldn't help but think that I could have been more helpful to them on their visit. No matter what I do in life, I always want to do it well. Back in Philly, Mr. Crowder used to say, first they have to see you, then always do something positive to make them remember you.

Having people around me and knowing that I am playing a part in making their day better by creating an atmosphere of peace, makes me happy. People remember you by the way you carry yourself and your attitude. The next week I had another celebrity. One which I had always liked Mr. Donald Southerland. When I picked him up from the airport, it felt like I was playing his costar in a movie that we were filming inside the terminal. He would walk over to me and say, you must be the man I'm suppose to see, and my line was "yes sir I'm the man."

After I grabbed his carry on bag, we started walking through the terminal towards the parking area. I like the

Dreams Lost and Found

feeling of walking though the airport with a celebrity. Seeing how they touch people's lives, by what people say when they see them. One lady walked up to Mr. Southerland and was so happy to see him in person, that she almost missed her plane. But Mr. Southerland, being the true gentlemen that he is, stood and talked to her as long as she wanted. It's good when a celebrity takes time to talk to a fan. It shows how they really are as a human being and that they appreciate the people that watch them.

After a while, Dav-el began to receive letters from people that I had driven. The letters stated in detail how professional I was and how they felt comfortable in my presence. The letters also stated that whenever they come back to town, to send Morris. I had quickly become one of the number one Chauffeurs at the company.

My personal list of V.I.P.s and celebrities was growing, and most of them whenever they came to Washington wanted no one else but me and that made me feel good about what I was doing. I've always believed that its not what you know but who you know. Over the years I've developed some good relationships and I'm thankful for that. As I began to drive more and more celebrities I became some what of a celebrity myself. Whenever I'd see friends or family members they would ask me who I drove that week.

Many times, depending on the mood of the celebrity, I would ask to take a picture with them. But I would never ask

Morris Bussie Jr.

if they were to busy or in a bad mood. I like to take pictures for two reason, because I could show my children and grand children, and because it let's the celebrity or the V.I.P know that they are still a star in my eyes.

The next celebrity I had the pleasure to drive was someone that was from my home town of Philadelphia and someone that I met when I was a young man back in Philly, Ms. Patti LaBelle. In the winter of 1999 Patti LaBelle came to town to do a concert at constitution Hall in D.C. Whenever she came to Washington she would always be traveling in her tour bus because D.C. was only two hours from Philly. She was staying at a hotel on Pennsylvania Avenue not far from the venue, Constitution Hall.

When I got the call from the office that I would be her Chauffer, it was like Christmas time but not for the reason of getting gifts, but for the joy and the feeling of that time. On the way to the Hotel to pick up Ms. Labelle for the show, I remembered thinking to myself, if she would remember the time I saw her in front of a grocery store in Philly, and she called me a handsome young man. I never forgot it, but she on the other hand, meets thousands of people sometimes in one day, so I didn't think she would remember me. I arrived at the Hotel thirty minutes early and parked the limousine in front of the Hotel. I let the doorman know that I was Mrs. Patti LaBelle Chauffeur. When Patti LaBelle came out of the Hotel, she was in Patti style.

Dreams Lost and Found

I have always thought of her as a one of a kind, down to earth person. I was standing at the rear of the Limousine as Patti came through the doors. She said hello to everyone that saw her. She stopped to sign some autographs and take some pictures. When she finished, she walked over to the Limousine and I said, "hello Miss LaBelle," while reaching out my hand to help her into the Limo. She said, hi baby, didn't you drive me before? I said, "no mama, but I did meet you before, years ago back in Philly." After I put her in the Limousine, I walked around to the driver's side, got in and headed to the Venue.

She was talking to the person that was with her. Suddenly she stopped talking and said to me, "driver, you said that we met in Philly," Yes ma'am, I was about sixteen and I was coming out of a grocery store in Mt. Airy, when I ran into you. I said, "hi Ms. Labelle," and you said, "hi sweetheart, with your handsome little self, I never forgot that." She asked, how long ago was that? I said it's been almost thirty years. We laughed and she said, "now you're telling my age."

Then she asked me if I was from Philly? When I said yes it was like we were old friends. We started talking about all the best places to go to get cheesesteak and the best hanging out places like Bellmont Platu. We talked about Mt. Airy and other places in Philly.

As we pulled up to Constitution Hall for her concert, her assistant gave me an all access pass for the show, and said,

Morris Bussie Jr.

"you are welcome to come in and see the show. Then Ms. LaBelle said, yea come on in. I said, "I would love to."

After letting them out at the stage entrance, I went and parked the Limo in an area they had for me near the stage door. I put on my all access pass and went inside. The rest of the night I was treated like a celebrity, because everyone knew that I was Patti LaBelle Chauffeur.

The show was one of her best, and she left it all on stage. After the show, Patti signed some autographs, and took some pictures with some of her loyal fans. Then we headed back to the Hotel. When we arrived at the Hotel, Patti asked for my business card and said, "all right home boy, when we come back, we are going to call for you." Please do I said, because if you don't, I'll be disappointed. Her assistant said, we keep our word.

As I walked to the back of the Limousine, there were a crowd of fans, maybe about fifteen or so. The Hotel security was standing outside to walk Patti into the Hotel. I opened the door to let them out. Her assistant stepped out first and whispered to me, good job Morris, then handed me a one hundred dollar bill and said, "Pattie likes you, when we come back to D.C., you'll be the first to know." If you carried yourself like a professional and do your job well, people will respect you.

Be yourself at all times.

Dreams Lost and Found

Be real at all times.

Be humble at all times.

Treat others the same way you want to be treated at all times.

First you have to look like somebody.

I have found that being a Chauffeur is an honorable profession. It gives you the opportunity to meet people that you would not meet in everyday life. It also gives you a chance to hear some great success stories that can help in making your life better.

One person that I really admire and respect for the work that he does with the youth is Edwin Moses. Even now, after his many days as a great track star, he gives his time and talent to the youth of the world, through work shops and different other activities through out the world.

I had the opportunity to drive Mr. Moses while in Richmond VA after they requested me because another Chauffeur didn't live up to his professional standards. When I first pulled up to take over the job, as they were walking out of the building towards the car, I stepped out, walked around to the rear door, opened it up, put out my hand and said, "good afternoon Mr. Moses , my name is Morris." I will be your new Chauffeur.

Morris Bussie Jr.

Right away I gained his respect. The person that was with him said, "finally someone that enjoys what they do. Mr. Moses said, "you don't know what we've been through today. For the next two days, they didn't have to worry about

Dreams Lost and Found

getting lost or smelling someone's arm pits. This profession is not a hard one. All it takes is common courtesy, common sense, and a little home training helps also.

The next V.I.P. I chauffeured was Paul Mitchell, the Hair Mogell. A Super nice individual with a lot of knowledge about his profession. I picked him up early one morning to take him to his meetings in Washington D.C. and Maryland. On the way, we had a casual conversation about the Hair Industry and how it was growing. I asked him how he managed to keep his products on top for so long. He said to me, "if you believe in your product and know that it can help make someone's life better, then you do whatever it takes."

Mr. Mitchell said, sure, I make a lot of money, but at the end of the day it's my name and reputation that's at stake. So that's why I strive to have the best products on the market. What I have learned from most successful people is that when you put your heart into what you love and believe in it, wealth will follow.

Sometimes you run into a celebrity that's going through some changes. It doesn't mean they're a bad person, it just means that they're human. So without giving details, I'll say hello, Mariah, its all good. We love you.

One of the highlights of my career was when I drove Johnny Cochran for the first time. Not only was he smart, but he was the coolest of the cool. When I first picked him

Morris Bussie Jr.

and his wife up from the airport, it was just like I had been knowing him all my life.

When you are good at what you do, and you're confident in a humble way, people see that right away. I believe that he and his wife noticed right away that I was a professional that made them feel comfortable. After they were seated comfortable in the Limousine, I got behind the wheel and headed to the Hotel. They were staying at the Willard Hotel one block from the White House.

I was going to be with them for the rest of the night, "and as directed." As directed is when your passenger directs you where to go for the time you're with them. When we arrived at the Willard Hotel, I pulled to the front entrance, parked and went to the rear of the Limousine to let Mr. Cochran and his wife out, but the doorman had beat me to it.

As they got out, Mr. Cochran turned to me and said, "Morris, we'll be out in about thirty minutes and we are going to Sweet Georgia Brown for dinner. Do you know where that is?" Yes sir, I said, o.k. he said, see you then. I waited in front of the Willard Hotel for about forty five minutes. I didn't mind at all, because after all, that was part of my job.

When Mr. Cochran and his wife came out of the Hotel, they were with a very well known African American news personality, who was going to join them for dinner at Georgia

Dreams Lost and Found

Browns Restaurant. I realized that night, that everyone doesn't handle success the same way. This guy had to be one of the rudest, most stuck up person that I had ever met. But no matter how rude he was, Mr. Cochran always showed me respect.

After that day, whenever he was in town, I was his Chauffeur. I was very inspired from the first day I met Mr. Cochran. I made a vow to myself that no matter what it took, I was going to work on building my own business.

Each time I had the opportunity to be in his presence, I learned a little more. One thing he said to me, I will never forget, its not just about us, it's about our children and their children. When Mr. Cochran died, I felt very fortunate to had the opportunity to know him, and the chance to benefit from his wisdom.

Morris Bussie Jr.

I believe very strongly that people are placed in your life to teach you something, weather they are good or bad. Mr. Cochran was one of the good ones. My life had turned into a mission to accomplish whatever I set my focus on.

I stayed with the company for another four months. During that time, I had the opportunity to drive many other big time celebrities, such as, Chaka khan, L.L. Cool J. Muhammad Ali, and Stedman Graham, who also works with youth.

Dreams Lost and Found

Many people know Stedman because of his relationship with the very famous Oprah Winfrey. But there is a lot more to the man than that. Stedman was in town to promote his book that was specifically for youth.

After spending the day with him and getting to know the real Stedman, I talked to him about my own son, who was having some difficulty with self esteem. He gave me an autographed copy of his book and said, it still takes a village to raise a child, so here's my contribution to your sons future.

When I first started as a Chauffeur, I knew that I would be good at it, because I'm a people person. Well, since I started, the people that I've met and the knowledge that I have gained, made me an even better human being. The dreams that were lost in my life, have suddenly been found and now I feel like there's nothing in my life that I can't accomplish.

At the beginning of 2001, I moved on to yet another company, Capital Limousine. Mike Yamada, a good friend helped me get the job. This company gave me the opportunity of a lifetime. Through this company I would find myself driving Royalty, but first there were more celebrities and stars.

The very first passengers I had when I started with Capital Limousine was a well known Restaurateur and wonderful human being, B. Smith and her husband, Dan Gatsby. They became one of my favorite couples. Whenever I saw them, they treated me with a tremendous amount of respect and would always thank me for my professionalism. B. Smith and her husband Dan would become my steady passengers, and I was always invited to eat at their Restaurant.

Another VIP I met while working for Capital Limousine was a humble man. At first glance you wouldn't know that he was a C.E.O. of a large Oil Company. Mr. Clarence P. Cazalot inspired me in more ways than one. Although this man had enormous responsibility and always worked on a

Dreams Lost and Found

full schedule, I never saw him get upset or disrespect any of his employees. Mr. Cazalot became one of my steady passengers also.

I loved what I did because it gave me an opportunity to meet so many great people, and live a good life. Not just for me but for the people that were around me.

"Always be at your best and your life will yield good fortune.

"Working with Royalty"

Capital Limousine was owned by three brothers from Syria, Sammy, Eddy, and Mike. Sammy was the older brother and the President of the company while Eddie, and Mike worked with the Chauffeurs. Like Dav-el Capital, had good clients, but the main account was 644, the Saudi Ambassador, who was a very wealthy prince. The Ambassadors residence was in McLean VA. It was a huge compound with the main residence, the guest house and a house that his two sons used when they were in town on school breaks. Prince Bandar was very well respected. The more I was around the people that worked directly with him, the more I learned about who he really was and how much power this man had.

Morris Bussie Jr.

Getting into the compound was an experience. Security was just as tight as the white house, but after a week of going to work there, the guards began to know me, and noticed that I was always consistently on time. I also gained a reputation for the way I dressed. First you have to look like somebody. What I had learned as a Young man back in Philly, was still with me, and I thank God everyday for the man I learned it from, Mr. Crowder.

I quickly gained the respect of the regular house drivers that were with the Prince from the beginning. The first assignment I had when I went to work there, was to drive some of the Prince's relatives that were in town from Saudi Arabia. All of them were Princesses and the whole day they would shop till you dropped. My job couldn't have been any better. From day to day I never knew where I would end up. All together there were six princesses. Everyday we would start out shopping, then have lunch, then more shopping, and back to the compound for a little rest, before either going to dinner or to the movies.

I learned that Saudi women are very particular, it was very rude to look directly at them. After spending three days with them, they became very comfortable with me. They would ask me about my family and about my life in America. One of the princesses became so comfortable with me, that everyday when she saw me she would walk up and grab my

Dreams Lost and Found

hand and squeeze it real hard, as she looked me in the eyes, and said Morris it is always, good to see you.

We also had security with us everyday. The Chauffeurs and security had to work together to make sure that we knew where each other was at all times. When the Princesses went into the Mall or into a Restaurant, their security person would be right with them. Whenever it was time for them to finish shopping, their security would call ahead to the Chauffeur and tell them what door they would be exiting. It had to be team work in order for the princesses to be taken care of properly.

We worked with these six princesses for two weeks, and when they finally decided to go home, they gave each of us a one thousand dollar tip. In two weeks I made five thousand dollars, and also had the opportunity to hang around Royalty. What an experience.

The next week I had the opportunity to drive Prince Fasil. One of Prince Baudars son Prince Fasil attended school in Texas, but once or twice a month he would come to Washington to hang out and visit with his friends. Before I started working as a backup driver for the prince and his family, one of the other drivers would have to drive the young prince when he went out with his friends for the weekends. I quickly found out why I was given the job of driving the

Morris Bussie Jr.

young prince and his friends whenever he was in town. My first experience with the Royal party animal was one of the most exciting times in my life.

Money was no object and everywhere we went, we were shown so much respect. It was the first time I actually experienced the power of money. I witnessed people just about breaking their necks to make this young prince happy. I think the thing that really stood out about him was his humbleness. This young man was wealthy beyond imagination, but just as his father, he treated everyone with respect.

One night after a long night of partying, he and his friends and the security team were walking out of the club, when a young homeless man approached him, asking for some money. Immediately his security stopped the young man, but the prince said "wait" let him come. By this time, the young man was afraid to say anything because of the Princess security. So he took the young man aside and they talked for about ten minutes. When they finished talking the Prince handed the man a hundred dollars and said, I hope this helps you.

The young man stood there in tears because he honestly had a need, for the money. After that night, my respect for this young Prince would be unbreakable. As time went by, I

Dreams Lost and Found

became known as Prince Fasil's driver. The young Prince was very generous to me. Whenever he came to Washington to hang out for the weekend, before he left to go back to Texas, he would give me a Thousand dollars. He always showed his appreciation for a job well done. For me it was an absolute pleasure to be able just to be in the presents of true Royalty. The Thousand dollar tips were great, but I would have given him the same quality service if he hadn't given me a dime, and he knew that.

I liked going to the Princes residence everyday to work because I never had to bring lunch. The staff was so large, and sometimes we stayed so busy, that no one had time to go out for lunch or dinner. Every day the kitchen staff would prepare breakfast, lunch, and dinner. If you were lucky enough to be at the residence at meal times, all you had to do was walk down to the kitchen. The meals were of the very best quality, and prepared by expert chiefs.

One of my favorite meals, was the one served on Friday nights, Steak and Potatoes with vegetables. The Steak had to be at least three inches thick, and cooked any way you liked. The Prince believed that a happy worker was a good worker, and one way to do that was to make sure everyone ate well.

All of the regular drivers that worked for the Prince were just like family. When I started as a back up driver, I became

Morris Bussie Jr.

one of the family too. Prince Bandar's driver was Mark, he was the number one driver and in charge of all the other drivers. Mark sometimes had a bad attitude, and when he was in one of his moods you didn't want to be anywhere around him. For the most part he was a pretty nice guy.

Then there was John and Mike who were brothers. John and I became good friends, and we would talk from time to time about any and everything. He was somewhat of a father figure, but the only difference was, I was black and he was white. We were family, from all walks of life. Mike, John's brother, was a big ball of energy. He was always in continues motion. He would smoke one cigarette after the other. Mike was a super intelligent person. He could make you tired just watching him.

Another driver that I became very close to was Al, he was the only regular house driver that was African American. He was a gentleman that had a lot going for himself. After getting to know him, I found out that he was also a pilot who had a lot of flying time. I was impressed, to say the least, with this group of drivers assembled to work for the Prince.

I felt right at home working with these gentlemen. From time to time, I was sent out of town to work with other Royalty. Who came to the United States for medical treatment. In

Dreams Lost and Found

late August of 2001, I was sent to New York City to drive a princess that was coming for treatment. On August 25,[th] I arrived in New York, two days before the Princess was to arrive. I was pretty excited to be working in New York. It was the opportunity of a life time.

Being in New York City was great, but being in New York City with Royalty was even better. The princess was staying at the Palace Hotel at 52nd and Madison Avenue. I and a few other drivers stayed at the St. Regis, which was a few blocks away. Most of the other drivers were from New York. My friend Shakor, was from Maryland and also had an apartment in New York City, in Harlem.

On the 26 of August, the Princess's security team, along with the drivers, got together at the Palace Hotel to go over the logistics of getting the Princess from the Newark Airports private terminal to the Palace Hotel in Mid town Manhattan.

That next day, on the 27th of August, the Princess's Plane landed. It was about 2:30 p.m., just before rush hour. We knew that if we didn't get her off of the plane and into the vehicles right away, it would be a long uncomfortable ride into Mid Town Manhattan. As the huge Saudi aircraft taxied down the runway and came to a stop, right near our vehicles, we all were standing there anxious to see what this princess looked like.

Dreams Lost and Found

Before they could get off of the plane, U.S. Customs had to board to make sure everyone's passports and Visa's were in order. By the time they were allowed to get off the plane, it was 5:15 p.m. The Princess had a large entourage traveling with her, but we came well equipped to handle it. All together we had sixteen vehicles, three Mini Vans, four sixteen Passenger Van's, five Cadillac's, three S.U.V's, and a Mercedes Benz, for the Princess.

When they finally started coming out, of the plane it was the children first with the nanny's, then the Princess aids, the cook, the shoppers, the money man, and his assistants. Then the moment we all were waiting for, the Princess herself. I knew from working with Royalty in the past, that it wasn't polite to look directly at them. But for a few of the drivers, that where from New York, they didn't understand that this was a serious issue. As we stood there next to the Vehicles, I kept feeling one of the drivers that were looking toward

Morris Bussie Jr.

the door of the aircraft. I informed him not to look directly at the Princess when she came thru the door, but he didn't listen.

When she finally walked though the door, we were all shocked. It was not the vision that I was used to seeing in a Princess. She was about three hundred pounds, and could barley walk. The driver that I told not to look directly at her, said, "damn and began to laugh." I turned away and ignored him, because I knew he wouldn't be there the next day. I got in the car as the security team walked her over and seated her behind me. As we started out for the Hotel, it was evident that this Princess had a major health issue, and on top of that, she wasn't a very likable person.

On the way to the Hotel, the driver of the Chase Vehicle proved to be inexperienced and wasn't boxing out or staying with me. This didn't make the security very happy, and it made for a security break down. The chase vehicle carries the security team. The driver of the chase vehicle has to be experienced and fearless. When we finally reached the hotel and assisted the princess safely up to her $4,000.00 a night suite, the head of security called a meeting for the drivers and security. The driver that laughed at the princess was automatically fired, and the driver of the chase vehicle was reassigned to drive the children.

Dreams Lost and Found

I also was reassigned to drive the chase vehicle, since I was the only one with enough experience. The head of security, Joe, also had worked for Prince Bandar before. He remembered me from what some of the other guys had told him about me. That's why it's important in life to always, first be a decent human being, then anything that you do, do it well. First you have to look like somebody. Then be somebody that people won't forget.

The next day, Joe, head of security, hired another driver from New York that had enough experience to drive the Princess, while I took over driving the chase vehicle. Most of the next day was spent at Mt. Sinai Hospital where the princess was having test done. Moving around New York City was a nightmare, especially when you are with a bad tempered Princess that does not understand that people are not going to move out of our way because of who she is.

After a few days, she became a little more pleasant on the way to her doctors visits. It was now early September, and the Palace Hotel was full of celebrities. Early Monday morning, after arriving at the Palace Hotel and checking in with the Command Post to get my assignment for that day, I got back on the elevator to head downstairs. The elevator went one floor down then stopped. When the doors opened in walks Mick Jagger of the Rolling Stones. At first I was speechless, then he said, "man what a nice suit." Thanks Mr.

Morris Bussie Jr.

Jagger. Then I said, I love your music. Thanks, he said. He probably thought I was a celebrity also since I was on the V.I.P. elevator. By the time we reached the lobby, we were laughing about the traffic in New York. As the elevator doors opened, Mick Jagger said, ok pal maybe I'll see you again." OK Mr. Jagger, it has been a pleasure.

The Palace Hotel has two sets of elevators. One for the public and the other for the V.I P.S. That way they can come and go in peace. Later that day, I ran into another celebrity, one that I had fallen in love with many years earlier, Mary J. Blige.

After a long day of shopping with the princess's assistant all over Manhattan, we returned to the Palace Hotel. The Hotel Manager had given us two parking spaces in the garage on the main level for the Princess's Mercedes and the Chase Vehicle. I along with the driver that was driving the princess, always had to stay with the vehicle's that were parked right next to the V.I.P. entrance. Every celebrity that was staying at the Hotel we had the opportunity to see.

As I was sitting there, recovering from a long day of Manhattan driving, a silver S.U.V. pulls into the garage and parks about five feet from my S.U.V. The driver gets out, dressed in typical hip hop gear. I knew it had to be someone in the music industry. Then he walks around and opens up

Dreams Lost and Found

the passenger door, and I almost lost it. Out steps Mary J. Blige. She was talking on her cell phone as she was walking towards the door. As I was sitting there with what had to be a look of shear joy on my face, she noticed me and stopped right in front of my S.U.V. By the time she got off the phone, I was out of the car, standing there with a big smile on my face. "Hi Mary I said, I love your music!" Thank you, she replied. "Make sure you get my new CD she said." "Oh I will" I said. She was just about to release her new C.D. which had the single Dancery on it. She walks through the door and get on the V.I.P. elevators. For the rest of the day, I was hoping that I would see her again, but I never did.

The next day, I had the opportunity to meet another celebrity. When I decided to write this book, I didn't want to portray anyone in a negative way however there are some people or celebrities that you just have to be honest about. What I'm about to say, may upset some people, but it's the only way to show how some celebrities forget where they came from. I understand that for celebrities, it's hard sometimes because there is always someone that wants an autograph, or someone else that wants to have their picture taken with them.

Lets face it, after all celebrities are human beings also and sometimes they just want to be left alone. But on the other hand, these people are loyal fans that have supported their

Morris Bussie Jr.

careers for years, and for them just to have the opportunity to see their favorite singers, or shake the hand of their favorite Basketball Player, makes them happy.

It was now Wednesday September 7th. After the daily routine of doctor's visits and shopping, we returned to the Hotel. The Princess's driver and I walked down the street to a Restaurant near the Hotel, where we ate everyday. After we finished our dinner we returned back to our vehicles, which were parked in the Hotel garage right next to the V.I.P. entrance.

After sitting there about fifteen minutes, waiting for Joe the head of security to call and tell us if we would be taking the Princess back out for the day. A Black S-500 Benz pulls into the garage and parks directly in front of my vehicle. As the parking attendant walks over to greet the driver, who was Amad Rashad. The passenger door opens and out steps Michael Jordon. I had heard from other Chauffeurs that Mr. Jordon wasn't very nice to his fans, but I was always taught never to judge a person from what others say about them.

It was an exciting moment for me to see a Basketball Legend, a supper star, up close and in person. As I stepped out of the S.U.V. and walked towards them, I spoke to Amad Rashad first, and received no response. First I thought he didn't hear me, but he looked right at me. By this time, Mr.

Dreams Lost and Found

Jordon was standing in the rear of the black S-500 Benz. As I came closer to him, I put out my hand and said, "how are you Mr. Jordon?" My sons and I had some exciting times together watching you play. As I'm standing there for about five seconds with my hand stretched out, all I could think about was, this guy couldn't be this big of a jerk!

I thought about what my friends had said about Mr. Jordon. All of a sudden, in the loudest voice, I said once again, Mr. Jordon Hello. He quickly abandoned his coldness when people walking by on the street in front of the Hotel, heard his name and turned to see if it was him. Suddenly he shook my hand and walked into the V.I.P. entrance. From that day on, I was no longer a fan. The joy of seeing one of my all time favorite Basketball Players quickly turned to anger. Unfortunately, that wasn't the last time I had the opportunity to witness Mr. Jordon's rude attitude.

The following year, back in Washington D.C., while standing near the front entrance of the Four Seasons Hotel. While I was waiting for a regular client and talking with the doorman, a guest of the Hotel and his young son were standing five feet away, waiting for the parking attendant to bring their car up from the garage. The young boy who had to be about ten or eleven years old, saw Mr. Jordon walking towards the front entrance and said to his father "look dad Michael Jordon." His father turned to him and said, "ask

117

Morris Bussie Jr.

him for an autograph son" while handing him the parking ticket and a pen.

When Mr. Jordon came near, the young boy said, "hi Mr. Jordon, may I have your autograph?" In the same rude way that he treated me months earlier in New York City, he turned to the young boy and his father and said, "No I don't give autographs." Then he turned and walked away. The young boy and his father stood there in disbelief. Then the father pulled his son close to him and said, "son that's o.k. that's one autograph you didn't need anyway." Then he turned to me and the doorman and said, "can you believe that a...hole."

As I stated earlier this book is not to make anyone look bad or to shine a negative light on anybody, but during my entire career, I have never experienced a ruder and cold way a supper star treated his fans. I just thought I would share that with you.

On September 8,[th] 2001, when I arrived that morning to the Hotel, I found out that another supper star was staying there, and it was none other than Michael Jackson. That day turned out to be one of the busiest days for us. The Princess had so many test scheduled for that day at Mt. Sinai Hospital. Later that afternoon she had a dentist appointment.

Dreams Lost and Found

Every location that we went to was close to each other, but the New York traffic made the day long. By the time we got back to the Palace Hotel, it was four thirty. As we turned off Madison Avenue and on to 50th Street, we were hit with a wall of people. It took us twenty minutes to go thirty yards to the front of the Hotel. This had put the Princess in a bad mood.

Joe, the head of security, got out of the S.U.V. and walked to the front of the princesses Mercedes. He tried to get the people out of the way, but didn't have much success. After five minutes, I got on my radio and called Joe, and said just let the people know that we are going to start moving very slowly towards the Hotel and they will know to move. As we started to move, so did the crowed. When we reached the garage, there was a black Van parked in the spaces that the Hotel had assigned for the Princesses Vehicles.

Joe was furious and had turned as red as a beet. He walked up to the driver of the Van and said, sir move this damn Van. The man got defensive and told Joe to kiss his you know what. At first we didn't know what was going on and why all these people were outside of the Hotel. Suddenly we remembered that Michael Jackson was at the Hotel for the next couple of days. It was already a night mare as far as traffic was concerned, the crowds were even worst. No one brings a crowd like Michael Jackson, it was unbelievable.

Morris Bussie Jr.

Those few weeks in New York City was one of the highlights of my life. In one week I had the opportunity to meet some of my all time favorite celebrities all but one was cool.

The next day the princess wasn't feeling very well, it was an easy day for us, except for the fact that there were about two Hundred people hanging around, trying to catch a glimpse of Michael Jackson. The Hotel had assigned parking spaces for Michael Jackson's vehicles that were right next to the Princess's vehicles. Although Michael Jackson was famous, the Princess had more money, so we had the better of the two.

As we sat there for most of the day, waiting for Joe to call with the game plan, I had a chance to get to know Mr. Jackson's security people and his driver. As big of a star as Michael Jackson is, I was surprised to find out that he only had two security people with him plus his driver. Later that evening, Mr. Jackson was scheduled to leave the hotel and make his way over to the Concert Hall. During this time, the crowed had grown to about five hundred people.

There were two security people from the hotel, plus Mr. Jackson is two. That wasn't enough to hold back five hundred screaming fans, most of which were females. Mr. Jackson's head of security, walked over to me and the Princess's driver

Dreams Lost and Found

and ask us if we would help keep the crowd back when Michael came out, we quickly said yes.

The crowd kept their eyes on the garage, knowing that any minute Michael Jackson would be coming out. Finally the door of the V.I.P. entrance opened and out walked the Hotel security. He walked over to the long black limousine that the hotel had sent to take Mr. Jackson from the hotel to the concert hall. One of Michael security people walked back over to us and said o.k. he's on the elevator, get ready.

As I walked to the garage, facing the crowd with my back to the Limousine, the V.I.P. door swung open. I could tell right away that Michael Jackson had just walked out. All of a sudden it got so loud I couldn't hear myself talk. I began to yell, stay back, get back, but couldn't hear a word I was saying.

One young lady was so determined to get to Michael Jackson, that she reminded me of a professional running back like Lyn Swan or Barry Sanders. As she cut and weaved, she spun me around until I was facing Michael. As I reached out to grab her I noticed Michael Jackson standing by himself in the corner of the garage, where everyone could see him. Although he was trying to please his fans, some that had waited all night to get the chance to see him, I felt it was not a good idea for him to expose himself to the crowds.

Morris Bussie Jr.

Even if we had ten security people, it wasn't enough. I grabbed the young lady and pushed her back, at the same time opening the door of the Limo and said, "o.k." Mr. Jackson you might want to get in now." He said, thank you I think that's a good idea. At that time, one of his securities ran from the other side of the Limo to help hold back the crowd that had suddenly filled the garage. As soon as Michael was inside the Limo, the driver started moving slowly. As the Limousine headed out of the garage and down the street, the fans were running behind. One young lady had gotten on the hood of the Limo and road it all the way to Park Avenue before getting off.

That was an exciting day in my life, and one I will never forget. Not many people can say that they worked security for Michael Jackson, but I did for fifteen minutes. It was the most exciting and exhausting fifteen minutes of my life. After that day, I thought about all of the dreams I had of being an entertainer. Looking at Michael Jackson, Mary J. Blige, and some of the other celebrities that appeared to be enjoying their success, helped me to want to find the dreams that I had lost. I knew it would take hard work and determination, but I was willing to do what it took.

I made a vow, once I got back to Washington I would start working on my dreams. I had become inspired again.

Dreams Lost and Found

Just like growing up in Philly but the only difference was, I was more focused and determined.

It was now September the 10th 2001. All of the celebrities had gone home. The only high rollers left, at the Palace Hotel was the Princess and her staff. We didn't have anything scheduled for that day. Most of her doctor's appointments were over. There was still a lot of shopping to do. That day was unbelievable, I saw so much money being spent that I literally got sick. Maybe it was because we didn't stop to eat or maybe it was the amount of money that I saw change hands, about Sixty Thousand dollars, to be exact.

The Princess's driver and I, along with the security were totally amazed. Joe, the head of security, turned to us and said, "my God she's shopping like it's the end of the world." We all laughed and said, maybe she know something we don't. We could always tell when Saudi women were about to return to their country because they start buying everything in bulk. If they see a pair of shoes, a dress, or whatever, they could never just by one.

I found out that they buy for family and friends back home, who wants to have something that comes from the United States. Finally, it was time to eat. The Princess must have felt generous that day because she treated everyone to lunch at the Four Season Hotel. After lunch, our day was

Morris Bussie Jr.

done. Joe asked us to stay around the Hotel in case the Princess wanted to go out again. About 6 p.m., Joe called me on the radio and said that I could leave, but I needed to be back at the hotel at 8 a.m. the next day.

My friend, Shakor, who was also working on the detail and was also from Washington, but had an apartment in Harlem and invited me over to hang out for awhile. After a few hours I decided to go back to my Hotel and get some rest. I still wasn't feeling very well from earlier in the day.

The next morning, on September, 11th I woke up feeling much better. I remember thinking to myself, "tomorrow is my birthday." I had never been in New York City for my birthday. I may never get the chance again so I'm going to do it up right. After I got dressed, I headed for the Palace Hotel. The day started out like any other day, but that would all soon change.

When I arrived at the Palace Hotel, I checked in as usual at the Command Post. The security agent on duty informed me that no one had called from the Princess's Suite as of yet. I probably should go and have some breakfast. It was now about 8:37 a.m.. Shakor called and said, "man I over slept." I told him not to rush because no one had called from the Princess's Suit. I walked down the street to get breakfast at the restaurant where we ate most of our meals. A half hour

Dreams Lost and Found

went by. A man that was sitting at the table next to me started cursing at his cell phone for losing the signal. At almost the same time, the cashier started yelling, "Oh my God," Oh my God. The man and I looked over at the woman who was facing the TV. We could see the woman's face, but the back of the TV was to us, so we couldn't see what she was so upset about.

The gentlemen and I both looked at each other as if to say, what is with her then went back to what we were doing. About a minute later I looked back over and to notice that she was still glued to the TV. Suddenly things got erie and strangely quiet. I got up from my seat and walked over to the TV. There were about six people standing around the TV. As I came closer I could hear the News person describing what had happened. When I turned to the screen, I could not believe what I was seeing. I immediately reached for my phone to call the Command Post to inform them of what was happening, but couldn't get a signal. I ran out of the restaurant and up the street as fast as I could. As I got to the entrance of the hotel, Shakor walks out of the garage. We both stood there in disbelief for a minute, looking towards Fifth Avenue.

At first we thought an airplane must have gone off course, but we quickly dismissed that thought because there wasn't a cloud in the sky. After standing there in front of the Place

Morris Bussie Jr.

Hotel, we decided to walk one block up from the hotel to Fifth Avenue, where we could see the Towers from 50th Street and Fifth Ave. It seemed as if life had come to a complete stand still. Just then one of the New York drivers walked up and joined us.

On every corner people were looking towards the Trade Center. Another plane pasted over our heads, at the time no one thought anything of it. Then out of the blue, a homeless man that was standing to the right of us said, that plane is headed to the other Tower. Immediately people that were standing with us told him to shut his mouth. The New York driver that we were working with, grabbed the man and said, if you say another word I'll break your neck. Then as sure as we were standing there, the second plane hit the second Tower. It was like a scene from a move. The only thing was this was real life. It was the worst thing I had ever witnessed.

Some people were crying, others stood frozen, while many others ran farther up Fifth Avenue to distance themselves from the situation. No one knew what to do, we didn't know if bombs would start falling next or what. I've never felt so helpless and confusion. The next few days were a nightmare. No one could leave New York and no one could come in.

Dreams Lost and Found

What started out as an experience of a lifetime, turned out to be a sad disgusting reality of what the world had become. How could people hate so much, that life means nothing to them?

On September 15th we were finally given the o.k. to take the Princess and her family to Newwark Airport. My birthday had come and gone, but it didn't matter. I was just happy to be alive one more year. When I got back home, my life had changed. I could no longer afford to be a procrastinator. Having dreams of doing this or doing that, and never getting around to it.

If I've never learned anything in my life before, there's one thing I know now, for sure. "Tomorrow is not promised. Follow your dream today" Because tomorrow is not promised.

"People That Have Made a Difference in my Life"

I've always had dreams of doing big things in my life, but somehow always got distracted. As a young musician, many years ago back in Philly, I had dreams of becoming a superstar. "If I knew then what I know now," I would be sitting on top of the world.

After being in the Limousine business for many years and having the opportunity to be around some very successful people, has made me realize that it's never to late to be successful.

Morris Bussie Jr.

We all know the story of Colonel Sanders, the man who started the Kentucky Fried Chicken, when he was in his fifties or Dave Thomas, the founder of Wendy's, who was also in his fifties. These men didn't let their age stop them from following their dreams, because they believed in what they were doing.

I was often inspired by some of the people I had the opportunity to drive. One of those people was Kevin Liles. I had no idea who this person was when I picked him up early one morning, in October of 2005 from a row house in Baltimore. At first I thought my office had given me the wrong pick up information, but later learned that he had turned his boy hood home into one of his many investment properties. After spending most of the day in his presence, I was surprised to find out who he was and how much power he had in the Music Industry.

Kevin Liles grew up like most African American youth in the inner city and had experienced many of the same hardships. But once he found out what he wanted to do with his life, he never looked back. He kept his focus and didn't let all the detractions take him off course. He started as an intern at Def Jam Records and quickly rose to become president. Kevin knew that if you really want something and you believe in yourself, you can achieve what ever you dream.

Dreams Lost and Found

Martin Lawrence was a big inspiration in helping to change the way I approached pursuing my goals and dreams. I had the pleasure of meeting Martin Lawrence on two occasions. One of which was at his house in Purcellville VA. One day after picking up a gentleman from Dulles Airport, he gave me an address to the location in Purcellville VA, at the time I had no ideal that this was Martins house.

On the ride out to Purcellville VA, I had somewhat of an idea that my passenger was in the movie business from his phone conversation. When we arrived at the location, after driving down a dirt road for about a mile and a half, I remember thinking to myself, I hope this guy is not a cereal killer. We were so far off the main, road, I was beginning to wonder if the address he gave me existed. Finally we saw a mail box, as I pulled into the long driveway and up to the huge gate my passenger said, "when you get to the intercom, let them know that Mr. Rogers is here to see Mr. Lawrence."

By this time, I'm thinking to myself this can't be where Martin Lawrence lives. After getting through the gate, we went another quarter of a mile before we reached Martin's house. It was like nothing I had ever seen before. This brothers house was so huge, it blow my mind.

Morris Bussie Jr.

Being in this business takes you to some of the most fabulous houses that you could imagine. I've had the opportunity to work with a Royal family at their home and other entertainers, movie stars, and many other successful people, but this guy had it together.

Martin's house was built around his very own Lake. Inside of his house was a basketball court, swimming pool, movie theater, and bowling alley. I was so impressed and so happy to see such a young successful African American male, I could hardly contain myself.

After their meeting was over, Mr. Rogers and Martin came out of the house. Martin looked just like he did on T.V. As I stood there next to the car, Martin looked over at me smiled and said, hay man "how you doing" fine Mr. Lawrence how about yourself as I walked over to shake his hand, he looked at me and said, you look familiar, did you drive me before? Yes sir I did, you have a good memory I said. I asked if he remembered my wife and her cousin that grew up with him. Martin said he remembered, and also added that she was fine, I said thanks and we shook hands again. Mr. Roger's and I headed back to the airport Martin Lawrence remembered where he had come from. Now he was successful and happy because he stayed focused on his dream.

Dreams Lost and Found

"The Weekend with his Royal Badness"

On March 10th 2006, I got a phone call from one of the many companies of which, I worked for from time to time. They told me that I had been recommended to drive a high profiled celebrity. They were coming to Washington D.C. to perform at a South East night club called Nation. The three day performances were to be held on Saturday, Sunday, and Monday nights. Normally I didn't work on the weekend. When they told me the artist was Prince himself, I said o.k., I'll make an exception.

On that Friday, before the three day event, I went to do some reconnaissance, to find out exactly where the club was.

Morris Bussie Jr.

Over the years, since I started as a Chauffeur, I made it a habit to find out all the details before hand. The best route to take to get to where you're going and what door or entrance to use. One other thing I've learned over the years is that the more you learn about the person that you are driving, the more you are able to serve them and fulfill their needs. Sometimes that's not an easy thing to do especially if you're driving them for the first time. In that case, the best thing to do is to be quiet and humble, speak when spoken to, say yes sir and no sir.

The most important thing is to be professional. After all, this is what you do for a living, so be the best at it. So many things I learned as a young man back in Philly, I still carry with me today. I'm thankful to men like Mr. Crowder and the old heads that used to stand on the corner and share real life stories and how to be a real and respectable man. They thought me how to carry myself.

When Saturday came, I was prepared to pick Prince and his assistant up from the airport. I got a call telling me that they wouldn't be coming in until the next day. For me, that was just fine because it gave me all day Saturday to spend with my sweetheart of a wife, Sylvia. I've always been a family man and anytime I have to spend with family, I love it. Prince's plane was arriving on Sunday at 6:29 p.m. It was a perfect time because we were able to get up and go to

Dreams Lost and Found

church Sunday morning. My new wife and I were married at our church one year earlier on April 23rd 2005 and we love it there.

So when Princes arrival time was delayed again, until Sunday evening, I was very happy because that ment that we wouldn't miss Sunday morning service. After church we went home. I did a few things around the house, until it was time for me to head to the airport.

On the way to the airport, I had to stop by the office in Sterling VA, to pick up an eight passenger Limo. After picking up the Limo and making sure it was clean. I went to the supper market and bought some fresh fruit to put in the back of the Limo. It's the little touches that make a difference from good Chauffeurs and great ones. Although Prince is a super celebrity, he came in on a commercial flight. Some people may think that to be a little crazy, being he's super rich. But after spending a little time in his presence, I found him to be a very responsible and conscientious person when it comes to spending his money. I also found him to be a very spiritual person.

We had a greeter at the airport to meet Prince and his assistant once they got off of the plane. When I arrived, I called the greeter to coordinate where to meet them once he made contact. When the plane landed the greeter made

Morris Bussie Jr.

contact with Prince and his assistant. He called me to let me know at what door to meet them. We had to time it perfectly because Raul, Prince's assistant wanted him to be able to get right in the Limo. I pulled around to the terminal with three minutes to spare.

As I'm standing on the outside of the Limo looking into the terminal, I first see Mark Lyels the greeter, walking towards me at a fast pace. Then I see Raul, Prince's assistant walking even faster, two seconds later here comes the man himself Prince. As he's walking towards the Limo through the main terminal, everyone that he walks by stops in amazement. Here is a living legend, an icon, walking through the airport with all of the regular people. When they got to the Limo, Raul his assistant, opened the rear passenger door and let him in. I was already seated behind the wheel as Raul sat down next to me on the passenger side. When Prince got in the Limo, he didn't say a word. One of the rules of the business is to speak when spoken to, so I didn't say anything. As we headed out of the airport, Raul reached over to shake my hand and introduced himself in a low voice.

One thing I wanted most on the ride into the city, was for Prince to be completely at ease. The smoother the ride the more relaxed he would be. One other little trick I learned over the years, is that people, especially celebrities don't like to feel that they're being watched. Whenever I have a passenger

Dreams Lost and Found

in the back seat, I always turn the rear view mirror up so there will be no awkward eye contact.

Ten minutes into the ride to D.C., Raul was on the phone making arrangements for someone to meet us at the Hotel, so that they could escort Prince up to his suite. Then Prince spoke for the first time and said, Raul, yes sir, Raul replied, make sure that they have some Lentil Soup in the room when I get there. Yes sir, Raul replied, again. I couldn't help but to think how incredible it was to be in the same Limo with the man that had some of the biggest hits in music history.

When we arrived at the Four Seasons Hotel, a young lady was waiting to escort Prince and Raul up to his suite. Before they got out of the car, Raul turned to me and said, Morris I'll called you when we're ready to go over to the Venue for rehearsal. All of a sudden Prince ask, is your name Morris? Yes sir, I said, then he said, I have a friend named Morris. I said yes sir I know, then we both laughed.

After that short encounter, I was more relaxed because I found that he was not only about business, but he was also a nice guy. They got out of the Limo and went into the Four Seasons Hotel. The doormen at the Hotel came over to me and asked Morris was that Prince? Yes I said, how long is he staying the doorman asked? Until Tuesday I said. I have always been cool with the doormen that worked at that hotel,

137

Morris Bussie Jr.

so they said I could stay parked in front. One thing any good Chauffeur should do, is get to know the doormen at all the Hotels. Be familiar with all the location of restaurants because at some point you'll need to know them. Ten minutes went by from the time they went into the Hotel.

So I took that time to check the rear of the Limo to see if I needed to replace any water that Prince may have drank. It always shows that you're looking out for their needs when you replaced the water they drink. My goal in anything I do is to do it well and try to be the best at it. I have found that people will always remember good service. They will never forget you if you are attentive and professional.

First you have to look like somebody. That's what I learned growing up in Philly. When people see you for the first time, they can tell almost immediately what kind of service you will provide from the way you dress. That's why I have at least thirty suits and twice as many dress shirts. When you're dressed good you feel good.

After waiting in front of the Hotel for a few hours, Raul called and said, Morris, we'll be down in five minutes. It was now 9 p.m. I was parked at the entrance of the circular driveway facing the front door of the Hotel. Ten minutes had passed, then I saw Raul coming through a door that was off to the side of the main entrance. He spotted me as

Dreams Lost and Found

he came through the doors and waved me over. Just as I pulled around, Prince was walking through the doors. Raul opened the rear door of the Limo to let him in. I stood on the outside and waited until Prince was safety seated in the rear of the Limo.

Since Prince didn't travel with a big entourage, I think he and Raul felt a little more secure with an extra set of eyes watching out for him. Raul and I got into the Limo with Prince sitting in the rear, and headed to the Venue, Nation. It was about a fifteen minutes ride from the Hotel. Lewis and Mr. Allen were already there. Lewis Gutierrez, a good friend and colleague, was driving Mr. Allen, who was the advice man for Prince. Wherever Prince had to go or whatever move he had to make, Mr. Allen would go ahead to make sure things were in order. On the way to the Venue, Raul and Mr. Allen coordinated where we should deliver the super star. Raul finished speaking with Mr. Allen and began to explain which way I should go. I turned to Raul and said, I came down yesterday and checked it out and talked to the manager, I know just where you're talking about. Raul looked at me and smiled, then said, "I like a man that does his homework.

Prince was in town to promote his new artist Tamara. I don't think anybody cared about the new artist, they just wanted to see Prince. I pulled the Limo around to the stage

Morris Bussie Jr.

entrance. Mr. Allen and Lewis were standing next to the huge tour busses that were parked by the stage doors, to add some extra security from people trying to take pictures. When I pulled up and put the Limo in park, Mr. Allen opened up the rear door. Raul and I had already stepped out and were watching out for anything that didn't look normal. Lewis Gutierrez had stepped behind the Limo and was looking down the alley to make sure the clubs security had put the barricades back up at the entrance to the alley. Prince stepped out of the Limo, looked back at me and said, "thank you" and continued to walk into the club, with Mr. Allen in front of him and Raul bringing up the rear.

Lewis and I stayed at the rear of the Venue with the Limo. Prince went in the Venue for about twenty minutes for rehearsal. When he came out, we headed back to the Hotel so that he could get dressed for the show. Prince and Raul came back out of the Hotel at 12:00 a.m. When they got in the Limo, Raul asked me to hurry back to the Venue. When we arrived back to the Venue, the DJ was still playing music as Prince prepared to go on. It was about 12:15 a.m. Prince and Tamara were scheduled to go on at 12:00 midnight.

Mr. Allen came over to Lewis and I, and gave us back stage passes, so that we could see the show. We couldn't believe it. To have the chance to see Prince perform was one thing, but to be backstage with him was a chance of a life

Dreams Lost and Found

time. As we walked in the rear door of the Venue, Mr. Allen stopped me and said, Morris come here for a minute." At first I thought to myself, what did I do? One of my trade marks over the years was to always wear a white handkerchief with my suits. It gives a distinguished and classic look. Mr. Allen said, "Prince noticed your white hanky and he needs to use it for his show." I said it would be my honor and pleasure. As I took it out of my pocket and handed it to Mr. Allen, Prince walked out of the dressing room and saw me give the handkerchief to him, and said, "thanks, I'll make sure you get it back." I said it's ok, I have others. He smiled with that cool shy look, took the handkerchief, and walked on stage.

The DJ stopped playing Lewis and I took our seats that Mr. Allen had chosen for us that were right on stage behind Prince. The crowd began to chant, we want Prince, and we want Prince. When Prince stepped from behind the curtain, the crowd erupted into a frenzy. Prince walked to the center of the stage, holding the handkerchief in one hand and fanning himself with his hat that he had in the other hand. Lewis and I turned and looked at each other at the same time, as if we both were thinking the same thing.

It was an amazing moment. I had been back stage with other artist before, but this was by far the most exciting. After Prince pranced around the stage for a minute or two so that everyone could see him, he walked over and picked up his guitar. He was still holding on to my handkerchief. I thought to myself, I can't believe it, the handkerchief that I was wearing is a part of princes show, now how many people can say that.

Lewis and I had the best seats in the house. I couldn't believe we were right on stage, sitting behind the drummer. The band was fantastic, but they would have to be in order to play with Prince. The base player was incredible and stayed right in time with the drummer, who was a female, but if you closed your eyes you couldn't tell. She could play circles around the best of them.

As Prince and his band began to play, Tamara and her backup singers walked on stage. Although the tour was to

Dreams Lost and Found

promote Tamara, the crowed was really there to see Prince. Tamara took center stage as her two back ground singers, which were twins, flanked her on either side. Prince in his usual Prince style, cranked out a funky sexy tone as Tamara and her back ground singers started to do a very provocative dance. The crowd, especially the men went crazy as the three women gyrated and twisted in their skimpy outfits. When Tamara opened her mouth to sing, it was evident why Prince was touring with her. She had a voice that captured your attention right away. No one knew who she was before coming to D.C., but she quickly gained everyone's respect. As Lewis and I stood back stage, I was tempted to take a picture of Prince while he was performing. Without being to noticeable, I held the camera up without putting it to my eye and snapped a picture.

After the show was over, Lewis and I returned to the Limo to prepare for Prince to come out. Raul called me and said that we would be going back to the Hotel first and then to a club called Indyblue on 7th and G Street. When Prince came out of the Venue, we put him into the Limo and headed to the Hotel. We arrived at the Hotel and just as before, Raul said, "Morris I'll call you when we are coming out."

They went in to shower and change for the after party at the Indyblue Club. Thirty minutes later Raul called, Morris we're coming down, pull the Limo around. Raul came

Morris Bussie Jr.

through the door and over to the Limo. As he opened the rear door of the Limo, Prince walked out of the Hotel in the badness, grayish purplish suit that I had ever seen. Raul put him into the Limo, then got in and we headed to the club Mr. Allen and Lewis were already there. Raul called Mr. Allen to let him know that we were five minutes away. When we pulled up to the club, the manager was waiting to greet Prince and Raul. It was now about 4 a.m. After they went into the club, Lewis and I stayed out side with the cars. About thirty minutes went by and the manager came out and offered us something to eat. We both were so hungry, and though that was the best thing next to Prince that we had heard all night.

Prince, Raul, Mr. Allen, and the band stayed in the club until 6:15 a.m. After taking them back to the Four Seasons Hotel, I headed home to get some rest for the next day. On the way home, Raul called me and told me to be at the Hotel at 6 p.m. later that evening, I said no problem.

When I got home, I kissed my wife and shared my experience with her. Sometimes the only draw back to the job is spending so much time away form home and your family. It always helps when you have someone that understands and supports what you do. After sleeping for most of the day on Monday, I got up around three o'clock to get ready for the second night of hanging out with Prince.

144

Dreams Lost and Found

Monday night was much of the same, the show and then to the after party at Indyblue Club on G. Street. This was one of the most amazing times in my career. Most people only see their favorite entertainers on t.v. or hear them on the radio, but my job allows me to get up close and personal.

On Tuesday March 14th, Prince was scheduled to leave. Mr. Allen, the advance man, went ahead to the airport to make arrangements to meet him at the aircraft. Raul needed to take care of the luggage. They trusted me to get Prince to the airport on time. As I was sitting in front of the Four Seasons Hotel, one of the doormen came over and asked if Prince was about to leave? Yes I reply, just as I said yes, Prince came through the door. The doorman opened the rear door of the Limousine and Prince gets in.

So here I was, just his Royal badness and I in a Limo headed to the airport. I couldn't believe it, I watched Purple Rain about ten times and now I got the man himself in the rear of my Limousine. On the way to Ronald Reagan Airport from the Four Season Hotel we pasted by some of the Monuments. He asked me to point out which ones they were. I gave him a little history on each of them. We talked about a few other things and I had an opportunity to let him know how much I appreciated his music. It felt like we had known each other for years. He may be a superstar but he's also one cool brother. When we got to the airport he said,

145

Morris Bussie Jr.

"thanks for the good service and I hope when we come back to D.C. we get you again."

I am convinced that if you are about your business people will notice. There were many other celebrities that I had the opportunity to drive once or twice. One of which was Brian Williams the N.B.C. nightly News Anchor. I had the opportunity to drive Mr. Williams on six different occasions, and everyone of them was an up lifting experience. Whenever I would pick him up, he always said, sir it's always nice to have such a professional driver.

Almost on a daily bases, I think back to what I learned from one of my mentors, Mr. Crowder, back in Philly, "first you have to look like somebody" but after they see you, let them feel your dedication and honesty. Over the years, I've learned that it's never good to talk a lot when people are in your presence for the first time, especially celebrities and entertainers. The only thing they are concerned about when they first see you, is can you do your job? After they see that you can, they are at ease and you become a professional person to them.

Mr. Williams is always in the moment. No matter where I would pick him up, weather it be the Airport, Hotel, or the N.B.C. Studios, he always had time to say hello or talk about how great life is and he would ask me how my family is. But

Dreams Lost and Found

when it came time to get down to business and we arrived at the studio, he always said o.k. its time to get my head in the game. Here's a man that loves life and all the things that are around him. When its time to get focused he get's down to business. You learn different things from different people to make your life better. My step father, Ronald Coleman, always told me you're never too old to learn.

There were many other celebrities that I had the opportunity to drive, like Star Jones, of the View, Rob Reiner, from All in the family, Donna Shalala, from the Clinton days, Ben Stien, from the Win Ben Stiens money show, Robert Rubin, ex Treasury Secretary, Clinton days, Mr. Cohen,

Morris Bussie Jr.

Record executive, Taraji Henson, movie baby boy, and Kirk Franklin, who is one of the most humble people that I ever had the opportunity to meet. One thing that I have learned from all of these people is "stay focused." Whatever your goals and dreams are, you can reach them if you stay focused. After being in the Sedan and Limousine industry for many years, working for someone else, I decided that it was time to think about my own company. As my wife Sylvia and I started making plans, I thought it would be a good ideal to continue working with the company that I was with until our business got off the ground.

On August 17th 2006, I had the pleasure of driving one of my all time favorite female entertainers, Miss Natalie Cole. When I first picked up Ms. Cole from the J.W. Marriott Hotel on 14th & Pennsylvania Avenue in Washington D.C., I thought it was going to be one of those bad experiences. When she and the promoter walked out of the Hotel and over to the Cadillac Escalade where I was standing, holding the door open, I said, hello Ms. Cole and got no response. After they got into the S.U.V. and we were on our way to the first location, I began to understand the reason why she may not have heard me. It had become obvious that someone had made an error in her schedule and she was a little upset about it.

Dreams Lost and Found

After we got halfway to our first destination, Ms. Cole leaned over and said, "hello driver I'm sorry, what's your name?" I told her my name and then she said, I didn't mean to be rude. We just had a little business to clear up. I said, please think nothing of it. I understand. It was a big relief knowing that one of my all time favorite female singers wasn't a jerk. The rest of the day was spent at the radio stations W.H.U.R, W.M.M.J, and a couple of others. After about eight hours of visiting most of the radio stations, I dropped them back at the Hotel.

The next day was another highlight of my career. I always wanted to attend a Tom Joyner Sky Show but never had the time to fit it into my work schedule. It was Friday August

Morris Bussie Jr.

18th I arrived at the J.W. Marriott Hotel at 7:00 a.m. to pick up Ms. Cole and the promoter. Ms. Cole came out at 7:25 a.m. That morning Natalie Cole was scheduled to make an appearance at the Tom Joyner show at Constitution Hall. Rubin Studdard and the Whispers were on the show. When we arrived at the stage door entrance, a crowd was there waiting for autographs. I got out to assist as if I was security for her and got her inside.

Once they were inside, I went back out and parked the S.U.V. Then I returned back to at the stage door. One of the security people that I was friends with let me back in.

As I was walking backstage, I ran into the Whispers. They had already performed and were backstage chilling. I walked over to one of the twins, who were just finishing a phone call. I wasn't sure which one it was, Walter or Scotty. As I stretched out my hand and said, "hay my name is Morris, Natalie Coles driver. I've been listening to you guys for a long time." He laughed and said "man you can't be that old," then I replied neither one of us is old, and we both laughed.

As I turned and walked towards the stage, I realized that I love my career. It gave me the opportunity to rub elbows with successful people. People that have gone through hard times, but kept their eyes on the prize and are now enjoying the fruits of their labor.

Dreams Lost and Found

Rubin Studdard was one of those people. As I was standing on the stage, behind the band, watching Rubin perform, all I could think about was the days of American Idol. As I was watching Rubin every night, I said to myself, this guy is going to win. Every night he kept his cool, stayed humble, but most of all maintained his focus. These are all good qualities for success.

After Rubin finished, Tom Joyner came to the stage and introduced Natalie Cole. The crowd erupted with applause and cheers. After Natalie took the stage, she let the crowds know about her new C.D that would be released soon and that she was in town to promote it.

One of the tracks from the C.D. was Day Dreaming, a remake of Aretha Franklin's songs. Natalie sung one of her hits from the 90's Mr. Melody, and the crowd loved it.

Then it was time to head to the airport. It's always hard to say good-by to a celebrity even though you're only with them for a short time. You get use to the excitement they bring to your life, and it makes you realize just how great life is.

The plans were under way for my new company. My wife and I purchased a new Cadillac that was built just for the business. It was equipped with a desk, foot rest, TV, video, seat warmers, lumbared, and window screen. It was a foot longer than a regular Cadillac.

As planned, I stayed with the company until the time was right to break away. Meanwhile, I was still being recommended to drive the high profile clients.

On September 19,[th] 2006, they asked me if I would like to go to Baltimore to drive P. Diddy. I said, absolutely. How soon do you need me to do there? I've always had a wish list of people that I wanted to drive, and P. Diddy was on it.

On Tuesday September 19th, I arrived at the Hyatt Hotel in Baltimore at 5 clock a.m. I wasn't due to be there until 6:15 but because I had a hard time sleeping from the excitement from the thought of driving the number one bad boy himself. I got out of bed at 3:30 a.m. and started getting ready. Altogether we had three brand new 2007 Cadillac

Dreams Lost and Found

Escalades, two turtle top Vans, and a huge Tour bus, I was the first one to arrive there about 5:00 a.m. Everyone else started arriving later. It wasn't until about 6:45 a.m. when we saw the first person from P. Diddy's entourage. The first person I met was a young lady named June. She was from a recording company out of Baltimore. As June and I were going over the details of the itinerary for the day, up walks Mr. Jerkins, P. Diddy's personal body guard.

I was impressed right away with how thorough and professional Mr. Jerkins was. He introduced himself to me, then asked if I would be the one to drive P Diddy. I introduced myself and said yes, I would be driving Mr. Diddy. He went through some details for the events of that day and asked if I would pass them on to the other drivers, I said, it would be my pleasure.

After going over the details with the other drivers and making sure everyone knew exactly where we were going Mr. Jenkins walked out of the Hotel and over to me and said, "Diddy and I will be coming out in about fifteen minutes." Make sure everybody is with their vehicle, o.k. I replied. I gave the other drivers a heads up.

At 7:15 a.m. Diddy and his entourage walked out of the main entrance of the Baltimore Hyatt Hotel and into a crowd of fans waiting for a chance to see the number one bad boy. Diddy was in town on a tour to promote his up coming new C.D., Press Play. The C.D. was due out on October 17, 2006. The C.D. was featuring some big names in the music industry like, Mary J. Blige, Big boy, Brandy, Christina Aquilera, Keisha Cole, Jamie Foxx, Nas, and Nicole Scherzinger.

After getting Diddy and his entourage into the vehicles, we headed out for the first stop which was W.E.R.Q. on Whitehead Road in Baltimore. We were scheduled to be there at 7 a.m., but we were running late. Diddy asked me to try to get us there as soon as possible. On the way, Mr. Jenkins turned on the radio to the station that we were traveling to. It was very exciting to hear the D.J. telling his listeners that he had a special guest coming to visit the studio and that he would be there any minute.

Dreams Lost and Found

Ridding down route 695 towards exit #17 that morning was one of the best rides that I had ever taken. Here I was going down the highway with P. Diddy in the backseat of my 2007 Cadillac Escalade, listening to a W.E.R.Q. radio station talking about him being on his way there. My first impression of Diddy was that he was cool and had much presence, but he also had that gritty street edge, in other words he could fit into any situation.

When we pulled up at the radio station, there was a small crowd waiting. The Baltimore City Police was on hand to keep the crowd back. Once Diddy was safely inside the Radio Station I began to plan the route to the next location. Half way though my planning, I was informed that we would be getting a police escort. It was already enough excitement driving one of the biggest names in the entertainment industry. Now to have the opportunity to race though the city in an official motorcade as P. Diddy's driver, was the single most exciting moment in my professional driving career.

After the Radio show, Mr. Jenkins called to tell me they would be out in ten minutes, and to make sure everyone was in place. I had already coordinated the trip with the Baltimore City Police department, and we were all set to go. When Diddy and his entourage came out and got in the Escalade, Diddy sat in the front seat next to me, and

Morris Bussie Jr.

Mr. Jenkins sat behind Diddy. We had four Police cruisers escorting us.

As we started out, the first thing Diddy did was put his own C.D. in. He was still working on some of the tracks that were not yet finished and I had the privilege of hearing them first. I thought the ride from the Hotel to the Radio Station was exciting and that it couldn't get any better, but I was so wrong. When we pulled out of the Radio Station Parking lot, the Police put on their sirens, and off we went. This was an unbelievable experience.

As we got onto 695, headed to Winston Middle School, the whole road opened up to us as we reached speeds of up to 80 miles per hour. It was almost as if I was in a movie. Diddy kept sampling one of his songs off the new C.D. The song seemed to fit the whole experience. It was incredible, a moment that I could never forget. Diddy had the stereo pumped up so loud that we couldn't hear the Police Sirens. The only time we heard the sirens was when he stopped the C.D. and started it again.

Once we got off 695 and onto the city streets, people would stop in amazement as if to say, I wonder who that is?" When we reached Winston Middle School, Mr. Jenkins suggested that Diddy stay in the Vehicle until they made sure everything was in order. As Mr. Jenkins got out to

Dreams Lost and Found

handled business, Diddy stayed seated next to me in the S.U.V. I wanted to tell him how much I admired his work and everything that he had accomplished, but the role of a professional Chauffeur is speak only when spoken to.

All of a sudden, he turned to me and asked, "are you from this area?" No sir I said, I'm originally from Philly, but I've been living on the other side of Maryland for twenty-eight years. Then he said, "so you must know your way around petty good then?" Yes sir I do, I said. Do you know where any good Soul food Restaurants are? Yes sir, I said.

Just then Mr. Jenkins came back to the S.U.V. and said o.K. they're ready, and Diddy got out. Diddy stayed inside Winston Middle School about thirty minutes talking to the students. When they came back out, Diddy hopped back in the front seat. As we started out of the school yard, I noticed some of the students that didn't have a chance to see Diddy in the Auditorium, were standing out on the school yard. I remember thinking to myself, how nice it would be if Diddy ran the window down on the way out so the children could see him. Sure enough he did. Those children went crazy. I don't know about you, but for me that's what it's all about, making other people happy. Sometimes it's not all about the money, but instead it's blessing people with your presence.

Morris Bussie Jr.

On the way back to the Baltimore Hyatt Hotel, for a press junket and lunch before we headed to D.C., was the same exciting ride. We were racing down the highway at seventy-five miles per hour behind a wall of police cruisers. After the press junket was over, we headed to D.C. This time we didn't have a Police Escort, as we headed down 295.

The people knew somebody important was coming by, as the huge tour bus, three 2007 Cadillac Escalades and two Turtle Top Vans stayed in close formation. The first stop in D.C. was the Four Seasons Hotel, where Diddy and his entourage were staying. At 2:45 p.m. we left the Four Seasons Hotel in order to make a 3 p.m. appearance at W.K.Y.S. Radio in Landam M.D. It was a long day but it would be an even longer night. Diddy had a grueling schedule, but he stayed focused and seemed to pace himself. At no time did he seem stressed or irritable. It was a pleasure to be in his presence.

After W.K.Y.S., it was on to XM radio in N.E. Washington D.C. I must admit that being in the company of successful people every day makes you want to be successful also. All of my life I've learned by listening and watching other people. Diddy and all the other successful people that I have ever had the opportunity to drive, have the same things in common. They think big.

Dreams Lost and Found

I spent two days with Diddy and at the end of those two days, I felt it was time for me to get into the game all the way.

It was time to see the big picture and expand my world, not just for me but for my family and friends. I never felt more positive about my future as I do now.

We all have a choice in life to except the things that life brings our way, or to follow our dreams and make life happen for us. Don't live everyday expecting a miracle to fall from the sky instead make it happen.

"My Turn"

In the first weeks of 2007, I was at a turning point in my life. All of the people that had crossed my path, left something with me. And something that gnawed at me day and night. It was a feeling of knowing I could do something and be something great. But I was stuck on stupid, then I realized "All of those successful people, are where they are at today because they followed their dreams." Yes they were probably stuck on stupid at one point in there lives also, until they realized "hay it's up to me how my life turns out." At that moment, I realized just how powerful my dreams were.

I remember one Sunday morning at my home church," Pastor Rev. St.Clair Mitchell told the congregation that God

Morris Bussie Jr.

speaks to us through dreams and visions, because he wants us to visualize within us a picture of our future. Then he said, "God also gives us dreams because of the affects it will have on us. Well, my dream was to have one of the best and classiest Limousine company's in the area. I decided to get down to business and make things happen. All I needed to do was follows the vision for my business and believe in my dream. I couldn't go wrong.

"I already had a few really good steady clients." Some of which talked me into starting my own company." People like Mr. Clarence Cazalot, the President and CEO of Marathon Oil in Huston Texas. This was a man that appreciated good service and would always let me know what a fine job I was doing. Whenever he flew in from Texas, I would always be at the private terminal waiting for him. Before I got his contract, he would tell me horror stories about having to wait once his plane landed, for his car to arrive and pick him up. Sometimes the wait was as long as thirty minutes. "First you have to look like somebody"!!! The first time I picked Mr. Cazalot up he and I knew right away that I would be his driver from that point on whenever he came to Washington.

In the Sedan and Limousine business, there are three things that are most important. Punctuality, service and knowledge of what ever city you're in. It's also important to

Dreams Lost and Found

look the part, and that is one thing I learned years ago back in Philadelphia PA. from Mr. Crowder.

When Mr. Cazalot stepped off of his private jet and into the terminal, "there I stood waiting," in a crisp black suit, white shirt, silver grey tie, and wearing a pair of black semi paten loafers on my feet.

I love what I do, and I also believe that "whatever you do, "do it well." So I decided that this was one dream that I would not let get away. I began to slowly build my clientele. The first was Mr. Cazalot of Marathon Oil.

Then came "Citi Group" and Mr. Robert Rubin, who was once the Treasury Secretary with the Clinton Administration. Mr. Rubin in my opinion is a great human being and a man that treats "everyone", no matter who you are, with the same respect!!! It was always an exciting experience when ever he came to town, because he still roles with his security people and they are all cool guys.

Another person who has supported my business from the beginning is also the President and CEO of a large company, "Mr. Craig Sincock of the Aufuel Corporation." A company that produces jet fuel for all of the major private terminals around the country. What I have learned being in my business, is that people gravitate to good service. No matter

Morris Bussie Jr.

who they are, they can be rich or they may be the average Joe. If you put your heart into what you do people will see it. Out of all the dreams I have ever had, I knew that I was on the right track with my Sedan and Limousine service. I love making people feel special and comfortable. It seems to come naturally to me. This was a blessing that I had to share with the world. It was "my turn" to let my dreams grow.

In March of 2007, a huge opportunity opened up for me. My friend Eric that I have worked with at Prince Bandars called me and said he knew of a very wealthy gentleman that needed someone to drive for him. He asked if he could pass my information on to his secretary. I said yes, by all means.

One week later, I received a call, then one week after that I began driving one of the wealthiest men in this part of the world, Mr. B. F. Saul, the owner of Chevy Chase Bank, the B. F. Saul corporation, and some of the most expensive Real estate in the world. It wasn't easy at first. Sometimes people who are that wealthy have some attitude problems. I have learned in this business that "patience has to be your best friend." Within a few short weeks, he understood that I was a professional, and very good at what I do. So after years of telling other Chauffeurs how to drive and driving them crazy, I had to let him know in a nice way that there was no need for his help.

Dreams Lost and Found

Chevy Chase Bank became my biggest money maker, bringing in $80,000.00 the first year. While it was a blessing, it also proved to be somewhat difficult, because I had other clients that wanted me to drive them also. I couldn't be in two places at one time. I realized that I needed to find some good chauffeurs to work for me, so I started my search. There is an old saying "your business is only as good as your employees." I wanted to find the very best people that had the same passion for what they did like I do.

At the start of 2008, we had four regular clients. By the time we reached April, we gained two more. Something was taking place that I had visualized years earlier. All of the dreams that I had were showing me what to do. Now, after finally following my vision, (my dream) and seeing the results, it was like living a whole new life. One thing I quickly learned about following my dreams is that you must "continually visualize your goal." Then you must be persistent and focused.

I'm always reminded of something the Rev. Jessie Jackson use to say, "keep hope alive." Whenever it seems like I'm becoming distracted or things look impossible, I visualize where I want to be two years from now and my dreams comes back into focus. It's my turn, my turn to be a blessing to someone else. My turn to help someone that is at a cross

Morris Bussie Jr.

road in their life. We all have a purpose in life. It's not just too simply get up every morning, go to work pay our bills, make a little money, and then go home and wait for the next day. There is a dream in each one of us. Something that we want to accomplish or achieve. Until we really do what is in our hearts, we will never be truly happy.

Our lives affect everyone around us, our children, spouse, mothers and fathers, people that see us everyday. You may never know the impact your life has on the next person so you have to be at your very best each and every day. "Follow your dream," stay focused, let your light shine, and don't let any human being tell you that, you can't do something. Whatever you dream, you can be. Don't wake up ten years from now wishing you had done something you know you should have done. I can remember one of the old heads back in Philly, when he used to tell me, "Little Brother" everyday that you wake up, you're in school!! You never stop learning, but it's what you do with what you learn, that makes the difference.

Dreams Lost and Found

Looking back, I have learned so much from so many people that I feel like a wealthy man, a man that is confident, a man that finally knows where he is going, and how to get there.

Whenever I have been in the company of a successful person, people like Rev. St. Clair Mitchell, Sean Diddy Combs, or Kevin Liles, or Robert Rubin, or any of the people that has influenced my life. I have always studied them. The way they interact with people, how they conduct business, and sometimes they would even share how difficult it was starting out. "This is what life is about." We are not born to just exist but to make a difference. To fulfill the dreams within us and to influence others to do the same. I'm following my dream, "so far" "it has taken me places I could never imagine." And I know I'm just getting started.

Morris Bussie Jr.

Hold on to your dream, and if you lose one, another dream is just around the corner. Remember God gives us dreams to show us our future.

Dreams Lost and Found

Dr. Martin Luther King Jr. said, "I have a dream," he saw the dream and believed in it. A young boy also believed, that one day he could be the first African American president of the United States. "Dreams are real." They give us an insight into our future.

Barack Obama, the first African American elected as President of the United States of America. (And I was there).

On January 15th 2009, I received a call requesting if I would be available to take care of a super star entertainer, that would be coming to Washington to take part in the Inaugural events.

Morris Bussie Jr.

My friend Less Anderson had passed my name on to Kevin Carter, and Eric Bowman, of Key Security Solutions. They said I came highly recommended as one of the best in the business. Once again it was paying off. What I'd learned as a young man has never left me and I'm thankful to men like Mr. Crowder, and my step father Ronald Coleman. "First you have to look like somebody." Every day when I wake up, I want to be better than I was the day before. But if takes character, commitment, and a love for what you do, and when you do it well, people will notice.

Jamie Foxx, was that super star entertainer, and it was my pleasure to be his Chauffeur for four whole days. It was another one of those unbelievable experiences in my life. The first experience was that this country had elected (<u>Barack Obama</u>) the first African American President of the United States of America. The second experience was that I would be spending the entire historic four day event with singer, song writer, actor, and comedian, Jamie Foxx.

Saturday January 17th marked the first day of this historic Inauguration. What made it even more special is that it was the 80th birthday celebration of Dr. Martin Luther King Jr., which was on the 19th. I'm sure that if Dr. King was alive to see this day, he would remember the speech he made when he said, ("I have a dream").

Dreams Lost and Found

This was a dream that seemed as if it was lost for a time, but now it's found. God gives dreams to show us our future.

Morris Bussie Jr.

Dreams Lost and Found

Morris Bussie Jr.

Dreams Lost and Found

175

Morris Bussie Jr.

Dreams Lost and Found

Morris Bussie Jr.

I believed God gave Dr. King the dream to know that (Barrack Obama) would be president of the United States one day, and that he also gave President Obama the same dream.

As I was driving on January the 17,[th] with Jamie Foxx next to me in the passenger seat, while listening to him say, what a humbling experience it was to be living in this moment and to be a part of this historic event.

It was a sobering experience for me. I began to take inventory of my life and what I was doing with it. Not only did I want to be the best person I could be, but I wanted everyone around me to do their best. Every celebrity that I have had the opportunity to work with, I have learned something from. What I learned from Jamie Foxx was that having your family around you was the most important.

Life is like a roller coaster, sometimes we're up and sometimes we're down. NO MATTER WHAT HAPPENS, ALWAYS HAVE A DREAM.

Printed in the United States
216854BV00001B/60/P